MULTIPLE
SCLEROSIS

MULTIPLE
SCLEROSIS

Nathan Aaseng

FRANKLIN WATTS
A Division of Grolier Publishing
New York • London • Hong • Kong • Sydney
Danbury, Connecticut

Photographs ©: Andy Levin: 80; AP/Wide World Photos: 85 (Khue Bui), 13 (Tony Esparza), 75 (David Longstreath), 77 (Seth Perlman); Archive Photos: 87 (Yani Begakis), 8; Corbis-Bettmann: 51 (Hulton/Deutsch Collection), 82 (Neil Preston), 39 (UPI), 18, 84; Courtesy of Howard Hughes Medical Institute and National Jewish Medical and Research Center: 46 (Barry Silverstein); Courtesy of The National Multiple Sclerosis Society: 36, 59; Envision: 27 (George Mattei); London Health Sciences Center: 41; Medichrome/StockShop/Anatomyworks: 16, 17 (Peg Gerrity); Nick Romarenko: 92; PEOPLE Weekly: 62 (1991/Acey Harper), 89 (1995/John Storey); Peter Arnold Inc.: 53 (Robert Holmgren); Photo Researchers: 55 (Will & Deni McIntyre), 24 (Meckes/Ottawa), 21 (Science Photo Library), 48 (John Watney), cover (Dr. John Zajicek/SPL); The Image Works: 56 (B. Daemmrich); The Weizman Institute of Science, Publications and Media Relations Department, Jerusalem, Israel.: 66 (David Harris); University of Wisconsin School of Veterinary Medicine: 70.

Visit Franklin Watts on the Internet at:
http://publishing.grolier.com

Library of Congress Cataloging-in-Publication Data

Aaseng, Nathan.
   Multiple sclerosis / Nathan Aaseng.
      p.   cm.—
   Includes bibliographical references and index.
   Summary: Describes the symptoms, diagnosis, effects, and treatments of the neurological disease known as MS, multiple sclerosis, as well as the stories of several well-known people who have this disease.
   ISBN 0-531-11531-3
   1. Multiple sclerosis Juvenile literature. [1. Multiple sclerosis.] I. Title.
RC377.A23   2000
616.8'34—dc21   99-34864
                                            CIP

Contents

Chapter One

A MOUSEKETEER'S MYSTERY AILMENT

"Why is this happening to me?"

That was a question Annette Funicello asked herself often. How did the ordinary daughter of an auto mechanic and a homemaker end up being America's sweetheart? So many lucky breaks paved the way for her success that she couldn't help thinking she led a fantasy life.

When Annette was a toddler, her parents decided on a whim to move from Utica, New York, to southern California. That move would open up a once-in-a-lifetime opportunity for Annette. As a 12-year-old, Annette performed in a dance recital in

Burbank, California. Unnoticed among the throng of proud parents, entertainment pioneer Walt Disney sat in the audience. Disney was on the lookout for appealing youngsters to star in his new television program. The dark-eyed, dark-haired Annette immediately caught his eye. After the performance, he introduced himself and invited her to try out for the show.

Skeptical of the entertainment industry, Annette and her parents tried to decline the invitation. But Disney was persuasive. Annette attended the audition and ended up as a charter member of *The Mickey Mouse Club,* which went on the air in October 1955. To her bewilderment, she immediately became the most popular of the Mouseketeers.

Annette Funicello appeared in *The Mickey Mouse Club* from 1955 to 1959.

Taking advantage of her fame, Disney launched Annette on a recording career, even though she did not think of herself as a singer. Using studio tricks to boost the sound of her voice, Disney put out thirty-two Annette albums.

While cancellation of the program in 1958 put the Mouseketeers out of show business, Annette's career continued to rise. Her wholesome, innocent, yet attractive appearance made her a natural for a career in front of the camera. She guest-starred in numerous television shows and made seventeen films, the most famous of which were a series of teen "beach" movies with costar Frankie Avalon in the mid-1960s.

Following her marriage, Annette retired from show business in 1965 to stay at home and raise a family. But she retained her appeal as America's ideal young woman, an image upon which advertising executives capitalized by featuring her in television commercials for Skippy peanut butter in the 1970s.

In 1976, Annette's fantasy world slammed headfirst into harsh reality. Late one night, while the rest of the family was in bed, Annette stood at the bathroom sink, washing her face. Suddenly, the room went dark. Her head began to spin and loud bells rang in her ears. In a panic, she lurched toward the bathroom door, hoping to reach her husband in the bedroom. But she tripped and fell face-first into a dresser, knocking herself unconscious. She cut her face so badly that the plastic surgeon needed 125 stitches to repair the damage.

"What happened?" she asked the doctors anxiously. Unfortunately, no one could answer her question. The doctors hoped that she had simply experienced a fluke malfunction of the nervous system that would not be repeated.

About 6 weeks later, Annette was checking her car's rearview mirror while starting to change lanes on a Los Angeles freeway when a large, black splotch suddenly appeared in her field of vision. When she could not blink away the blind spot, she pulled over to the shoulder.

"Come on! What is going on here!" she cried. No further symptoms appeared, so Annette cautiously made her way home. She sought out a *neurologist,* a doctor who specializes in concerns of the nervous system. The blind spot disappeared, however, and the neurologist found nothing to explain the phenomenon. He could only guess that the problem might have something to do with the blow to the head she had suffered 6 weeks earlier.

The two mysterious episodes left Annette bewildered and unsure of what to expect. But as years passed without further such occurrences, she began to feel more at ease. Perhaps those two incidents were flukes—temporary malfunctions. Annette went about her normal business, appearing in occasional television shows as a guest star and in a Mickey Mouse Club reunion special.

In 1987 she agreed to star in an updated version of one of her old beach movies. As she was reading through the script to memorize her lines, the type appeared blurry to her. Approaching her forty-fifth birthday, she wrote off the problem as simply a sign of aging and corrected it with stronger prescription lenses. But "age" soon brought a nagging series of other health problems. For example, she felt a cold tingling in her feet and had trouble keeping her balance in the sand. The more it happened, the more she worried, but she kept her concern to herself. When her costar had to help her up from a sitting position, Annette simply laughed about her clumsiness.

Annette's eyesight deteriorated so quickly that she needed a new prescription for her glasses within a few weeks. This alerted her eye doctor that something beyond the aging process was taking place. He referred Annette to a neurologist who put her through a series of tests. One of these tests was *magnetic resonance imaging* (MRI), which involved lying on a conveyor belt and sliding into what she described as a metal, space-age capsule, wearing something like a football helmet on her head. For 45 minutes she heard strange pounding noises as the machine collected images of her nervous system.

A few days later, the neurologist showed her a composite photograph of her brain taken by the MRI unit. Several areas of bright spots appeared on her brain. These, the doctor told her, indicated a nonfatal illness known as multiple sclerosis, often called MS.

Although Annette was initially relieved that her problem was not caused by a deadly tumor, she had no idea what MS was. Adding to her confusion, the doctors could give her only a rough idea of what might happen as the disease progressed. MS, she was told, is a disease that affects different people in vastly different ways. Some experience only minor symptoms while others lose bladder control and the ability to walk, see, and feel. No one could predict exactly what lay in store for Annette.

Fearing the unknown, Annette simply pretended that the disease did not exist. She refused to read any literature on the subject. That, she says now, was a mistake. She advises anyone diagnosed as having MS to read as much on the subject as they can.

Not wanting to worry people over a disease that might or might not show obvious symptoms, she told only her mother, husband, and children that she had MS. She tried to ease her children's concerns by calmly telling them when she was experiencing an MS problem, such as a foot falling asleep while she was watching television. Otherwise, she did not allow MS to affect her life.

In the back of her mind, however, dread lingered. A further attack could come at any moment, and she had no way of guessing when it would occur or what form it might take. Fear of an embarrassing incident caused her to decline making a follow-up beach film with Frankie Avalon.

But by 1989, when no serious problems had appeared, she decided to set aside her fears. She agreed to go on a nationwide singing tour with Avalon. At first she had no trouble disguising her illness and the occasional loss of balance and blurred eyesight that went with it. But gradually, more incidents occurred. At times her legs gave out on her and she needed to lean on an arm or a cane for support when she walked. Her father, and others, began asking her what was wrong. Annette explained away her MS symptoms by claiming that her many years of dancing had taken their toll on her legs.

Toward the end of the tour in 1991, her symptoms were becoming glaringly obvious. On one occasion, she came down with a virus that left her unable to walk at all for several days. Her cover-ups and excuses became more elaborate and she needed them so often that she had trouble remembering what story she had told to whom. Still, she refused to admit to her illness. "People always thought nothing bad ever happens to Annette," she recalls. "And I didn't want to disappoint them."[1] Nor did she want pity from her fans.

Early in 1992, Annette went out to eat at a restaurant with friends. Her balance and coordination were terrible that evening, but, as usual, she tried to laugh it off. One of her son's friends saw her. The next day he told her son that he had seen Annette falling-down drunk at the restaurant. Gossip reporters picked up the scent of a scandal and began asking questions around her neighborhood. Was it true that the innocent, wholesome Mouseketeer was an alcoholic? Embarrassed by the rumors and hearing that the tabloids were preparing stories about her, Annette finally decided to go public. She called a reporter from *USA Today* and spilled out the story of her MS. Then she held her breath while she waited for the public reaction.

To her surprise and relief, the public responded with an outpouring of support and encouragement. Annette was swamped with requests for appearances and endorsements. She marketed her own line of teddy bears and perfume, wrote an autobiography, and appeared in a film version of her book.

By the mid-1990s, Annette had difficulty walking. Frequently, she relied on a wheelchair to get around. She had considerable trouble keeping her balance, her handwriting was shaky, and she had trouble reading. Even the simple act of speaking required great concentration. She had to watch her overall health carefully. Illness, exhaustion, and stress can

Annette Funicello, center, poses with the three actresses who portrayed her in *A Dream Is a Wish Your Heart Makes*.

aggravate symptoms in people with MS. When she was filming her autobiographical film *A Dream Is a Wish Your Heart Makes*, the hot lights in front of the camera caused her body to "shut down," as she put it. "The next day, they packed my legs and back in ice to do a scene. I did just fine."[2] This is because some people with MS are heat sensitive, and raising their body temperature may temporarily worsen MS symptoms.

Like many people with MS, Annette has days when the disease barely affects her and other days when the symptoms are so unbearable that she asks in anguish the question she once asked in gratitude, "Why is this happening to me?"[3] She longs for some bit of medical magic that will make her problems go away. She has heard people recommend all kinds of treatments, from exotic diets and massive doses of drugs to untested medical appliances. Her husband, Glen, has traveled around the United States checking on possible treatments. Annette has tried a wide range of these, including steroids, herbal medicines, vitamins, and acupuncture. None has been effective.

Annette also knows that MS, in some cases, suddenly goes away without any apparent cause, never to return. In 1993, she had hopes that such a miracle was happening to her. She awoke one day with virtually no symptoms and could walk without the use of a cane. But the recovery was short-lived. Before long, all her symptoms returned.

Like most MS patients, Annette had to learn to deal with the cycle of uncertainty, hope, and discouragement. She discovered that, rather than sitting around waiting for a cure, she was far better off focusing on how to live with the disease to the best of her ability. "I really enjoy being busy," she says. "Especially having MS, it's better. When I have a bad day, I don't have time to think about it."[4]

Annette Funicello will face many challenges in the years ahead. She will continue to wince through periods in which she cannot help but ask, "Why me?" But she has not let MS prevent her from living a productive and happy life. She has decided to use her celebrity status and her positive attitude to raise public awareness about MS. Annette has shown that, in her own words, "life does not have to be perfect to be wonderful."[5]

Chapter Two

WHAT IS MULTIPLE SCLEROSIS?

Have you ever seen a flickering light-bulb in a living-room lamp or a bath-room fixture? When you flick the switch, the light may flash on for a fraction of a second and then go off. Sometimes, if you keep turning the switch on and off, the light eventually stays on. Or it may go on for several minutes and then flutter or go out altogether.

The problem is caused by a poor connection. A glitch in the wiring interrupts the flow of electricity to the light, though it does not stop all of the electrical flow and in fact sometimes allows the light to perform perfectly well. There is no way to predict exactly when and how this glitch will affect the lightbulb.

That is basically what happens to a person with MS. The human nervous system may be thought of as a complex electrical system. *Nerve fibers* act like wires connecting the muscles and sensory organs to the brain and spinal cord. Some of these fibers are less than a millimeter in length; some may extend several feet. The brain and spinal cord issue instructions to the muscles via electrical impulses that travel through these nerve

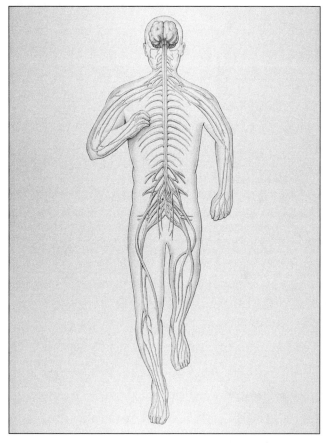

Nerve fibers carry messages in the form of electrical impulses to and from the brain.

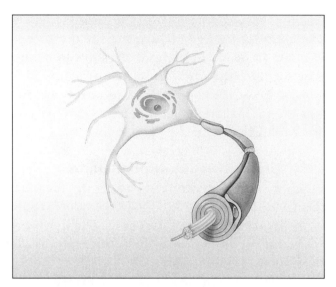

The nerve fibers in your body are surrounded by a myelin sheath made of fat and protein.

fibers and information from the sensory organs travels back to the brain to be processed. The electrical nerve impulses move quickly—at about 225 miles (362 km) per hour. For muscles to act properly and for the brain to collect information accurately from the sensory organs, the nerve connections must be solid.

Like any electrical wiring, the nerve fibers must be insulated by a material that does not conduct electricity. This insulation keeps the electrical activity contained and protects the wires or nerves from damage that might interrupt the flow of electricity. Human nerves are insulated by sheaths of *myelin,* a material made of fat and protein. If the myelin insulation becomes frayed or otherwise damaged, the flow of nerve impulses may be slowed down, altered, or interrupted. This means that muscles will not receive proper instructions and so will not perform normally. Information traveling from the sensory organs back to the brain also becomes garbled.

This is what happens in MS. It is a disease of the central nervous system in which the flow of electrical impulses from the brain and spinal cord to muscles and sensory organs becomes impaired because of damage to the myelin insulation.

The name "multiple sclerosis" refers to two main features of the disease. The destruction of myelin causes hardened patches, or scleroses, to appear in the brain and the spinal cord. Multiple refers to the fact that these patches are usually numerous and widespread.

Discovering Multiple Sclerosis

Prior to the nineteenth century, MS was generally unknown to the medical world, though there may have been unrecognized cases of the disease well before that time. The diary of a Dutch woman living in the fifteenth century, for example, describes symptoms similar to those of MS.

Jean Cruveilhier, a professor at the University of Paris, was the first medical professional to detect signs of the disease.

A French scientist named Jean Cruveilhier was the first person to notice patches now associated with MS along a person's central nervous system.

While performing an autopsy (a medical examination of a body to determine cause of death) in 1835, Cruveilhier discovered small white and brown patches scattered throughout the subject's central nervous system. Other medical examiners began finding similar patches in other subjects around the same time.

But, no one was able to link these patches to a specific health problem.

Meanwhile, a German physician named Friedrich Theodor von Frerichs began treating several patients who developed partial paralysis. He observed that this condition appeared to strike young adults, whose coordination sometimes grew steadily worse over a period of many years. In 1849, von Frerichs began diagnosing patients exhibiting this symptom as having a distinct disease.

The link between the disease reported by von Frerichs and the patches discovered by Cruveilhier was not widely recognized by the medical profession until 20 years later. On March 14, 1869, Jean-Martin Charcot, a highly respected French neurologist who specialized in conditions of paralysis, presented a paper to the French Biological Society. In it, he described in detail the symptoms of this paralyzing illness in three patients, one of whom was his housekeeper. Charcot's reputation was so great that this illness, which became known as multiple sclerosis, was accepted by the medical community. Even so, the term multiple sclerosis did not appear in medical literature until nearly a decade later.

While doctors have long accepted that multiple sclerosis results from disruptions of nerve impulses due to the scattered hardened patches, the cause of the patches themselves has been debated over the years. Cruveilhier originally thought they were caused by a body's inability to sweat properly. As recently as the 1960s, many medical experts blamed the problem on poor blood circulation in the central nervous system.

In the past 20 years, medical researchers have discovered that the hardened patches, now known as *plaques*, are damaged pieces of myelin. Although they still have many questions about the nature of multiple sclerosis, researchers have determined how myelin is destroyed in people with MS. The actual attack against the myelin is made, not by a bacteria, protozoan, yeast, or virus, but by the body's own immune system, which normally wards off infection and disease. In other words, MS is a case of mistaken identity. Understanding how this happens requires a basic knowledge of the human immune system.

The Immune System: The Body's Defender

In the late nineteenth century, a number of scientists, including Louis Pasteur of France and Robert Koch of Germany, proved that some human diseases are caused by tiny organisms called bacteria. Researchers soon realized that the human body provides an ideal environment for a host of other tiny invaders, including protozoans and viruses.

When these microscopic invaders penetrate the body through air passages or an open wound, they find a warm, moist home filled with readily available nutrients. Some of these invaders reproduce so rapidly that if they are not stopped, they can quickly overrun the body—causing sickness or death.

The scientists noticed that some people recover from attacks by these invaders, but they weren't sure why. What stopped the tiny creatures from overwhelming these people?

In 1888, a Russian microbiologist named Elie Metchnikoff provided the first evidence that the human body actively defends itself against microscopic invaders. While studying blood under a microscope, Metchnikoff detected a number of large, colorless cells. Unlike the red blood cells, which carry oxygen throughout the body, these larger white blood cells act like tiny hunters. They wander through the bloodstream capturing and engulfing bacteria and other invaders. Metchnikoff named these white blood cells phagocytes, which means "cells that eat."

Metchnikoff's discovery of phagocytes showed that the body has a built-in defense system for fighting off foreign par-

Elie Metchnikoff was the first person to describe phagocytes—white blood cells that capture and engulf foreign particles.

ticles. Emil von Behring of Germany then showed how astoundingly complex this system is. He studied the blood of people who had survived a deadly disease called diphtheria. Diphtheria is caused by a poison, or toxin, produced by bacteria. Behring found that the blood of survivors contains a chemical capable of neutralizing the diphtheria toxin. He called the chemical an antitoxin. Even more intriguing, Behring found that only people who had contracted diphtheria had this antitoxin in their blood. Thus, he concluded that when the body is exposed to diphtheria toxin, it manufactures the antitoxin to defend itself.

Researchers soon discovered other weapons in the body's chemical defense arsenal. Some of these materials could neutralize toxins; others destroyed bacteria or viruses. All of them were most noticeable immediately after an infection. Since some of the chemicals did not target toxins, scientists could not call them antitoxins. Instead, they gave all of these agents the general name *antibodies.*

In the 1930s, researchers discovered that antibodies consist of unusually shaped protein molecules. In fact, the molecules on the surface of an antibody seem to be a mirror image of the molecules on the surface of a particular disease-causing microorganism or toxin. Eventually, researchers concluded that antibodies search for their targets by comparing their own surface molecules with those of passing organisms. Known as *surface markers,* the molecules on the surface of invaders act like name tags, broadcasting their identity to antibodies.

When an antibody comes into contact with its target intruder, it binds to its enemy. The antibody and the intruder fit together like a key fits a lock. As long as the antibody stays attached to the disease organism, the intruder can do no harm. Once an antibody "marks" an invading organism, a phagocyte can easily find and devour the enemy.

In 1948, researchers isolated the group of white blood cells that manufacture antibodies and named them B-lymphocytes, or B-cells for short. B-cells are made in the bone marrow. In the 1960s, scientists discovered another type of lymphocyte. Because these lymphocytes are manufactured in the thymus—a gland near the neck—they are called *T-cells.* Although lymphocytes and phagocytes are both kinds of white blood cells, they look very different and have different functions.

The Trillion-Soldier Army

In recent years, scientists have determined that the immune system is a marvelously complex defense network that involves one of every 100 body cells, roughly a trillion total cells. This enormous arsenal of cells is controlled by a vast communications network that has two key features:

- A memory system that cells can call upon to distinguish harmful invaders from necessary body molecules.
- A specific response to ensure that *antigens* are destroyed without damaging innocent-bystander cells.

Scientists are not certain how the body makes up its list of what is foreign and what is "self." The logical time for it to take inventory would be before birth, when the fetus is shielded from external antigens and there are no harmful molecules present. Indeed, scientists believe that white blood cells circulate through the fetus before birth and catalog the body's molecules. Then, after birth, the immune cells check all the molecules they encounter against this original list.

The cells of the immune system act as a team to identify and attack foreign invaders. A group of B-cells called *antigen-presenting cells* (APCs) travels through the body in search of intruders. When they encounter a cell or particle, they break off a piece of it and display it on their outer surface. These APCs do not judge whether the cell or particle is harmful or not; they merely present the evidence. Meanwhile, T-cells, which can wriggle through the spaces between cells and challenge every entity they meet (from protein molecule to dust particle), are also on patrol. When a T-cell passes an APC, it examines the surface markers to see if the material has come from one of the body's own cells or an unauthorized invader.

A particular T-cell can usually recognize only one kind of antigen. The human body contains millions of different T-cell types, each on the lookout for a particular enemy. A T-cell recognizes its assigned enemy by fitting the fragment displayed by the APC into a receptor on its own surface. Just as the shape of an antibody matches the shape of an antigen, the shape of T-cell's receptor matches the shape of the antigen fragment. Much like the ignition on a car, the T-cell receptor can be turned on by only one key. The vast majority of surface fragments that a T-cell tests will not fit into the receptor.

If a surface fragments does not fit, the T-cell moves on to challenge another fragment held up by another APC. But if the fragment does fit, the T-cell knows it has encountered an enemy and sounds an alarm. The entire immune system roars to life.

Some of the T-cells, known as killer T-cells, can destroy the antigen themselves. Other T-cells stimulate an inflammatory reaction at the infection site. They release chemicals that cause tiny blood vessels to swell so that large antigen-eating phago-cytes can more easily enter the area. And to make the environment more uncomfortable for the invader, the immune system stimulates fluid production in the tissues, causing the body's temperature to rise.

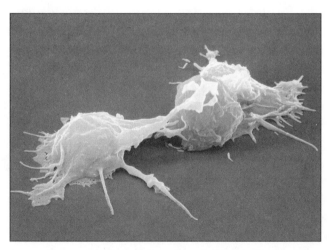

This image, which was taken through a scanning electron microscope, shows a killer T-cell (left) attacking a cancer cell (right).

Still other T-cells leave the reaction site, carrying with them a pattern of the antigen's surface markers. They enter the lymph channels, a specialized network of passageways that only immune system cells travel through, and search for B-cells to manufacture the one antibody that will be effective against the invader. When the T-cells chemically activate the proper B-cells, they turn into antibody factories, churning out a vast supply of the appropriate antibody.

T-cells begin reproducing rapidly so that more T-cells are available to turn on more B-cells. Within a short period of time, the immune system is spewing out a flood of antibodies that swarm over the infection site and attach themselves to the surface markers of the invaders. In addition to neutralizing the antigens and flagging them for easy recognition, antibodies also cause antigens to clump together to create larger targets for phagocytes and other killer immune cells. Immune cells that have been damaged add more firepower to the attack by releasing chemicals that attract greater numbers of cell eaters to the infected area.

Once the invaders have been defeated and the danger of infection is over, the T-cells release chemicals that shut down the immune reaction. Even after the attack is over, B-cells continue to manufacture smaller numbers of antibodies. The next time the invader penetrates the body, the immune system will be ready for it. Instead of struggling for days to overcome a rapidly reproducing invader, the existing antibodies may be able to stop an infection before it ever gets started.

The immune system is usually highly effective in warding off disease. The lock-and-key method of identification ensures that the system targets only the invading antigen. The body quickly builds up a massive supply of the proper antibody. It does not waste time and energy manufacturing unneeded antibodies. Finally, even after the immune system shuts down most of its attack, it maintains a line of defense as insurance against future invasions.

Immune systems vary from person to person. Some people have such effective immune systems that they are able to fight off the most widespread diseases. Even when cold and flu epidemics sweep through their communities, they rarely get sick. Other people seem to catch whatever "bug" is going around. Their immune systems are less efficient at fighting infection. As people grow older, their immune systems gain experience with different antigens. As a result, adults are immune to more illnesses than children. On the other hand, people's immune systems also tend to wear out or break down as they get older. That makes the elderly more susceptible to illnesses such as cancer.

What Can Go Wrong with the Immune System

As marvelously sophisticated as the human immune system is, it is neither invincible nor foolproof. In the relentless attempt to gain access to the human body, bacteria and viruses have evolved elaborate strategies for defeating or bypassing the immune system. Over the course of a few generations, they may alter the shape of their surface receptors. This means that a flu virus that attacks today may be quite different from the ancestor virus that attacked the same person years earlier. If the change is significant enough, the antibodies built up against the original virus may no longer work and the person becomes sick again.

Sometimes, the immune system actually does more harm than good, particularly when it cannot easily distinguish between foreign molecules that cause damage and those that do not. In such cases, immune systems sometimes attack a harmless substance, causing uncomfortable symptoms in the process.

If the immune system attacked every foreign particle that enters the body, we could not survive. Food, for example, contains many molecules that the immune system identifies as foreign. Yet those molecules are necessary to maintain life. What does the immune system do with these suspect invaders? In most cases, it ignores foreign particles that pass through the digestive system. But sometimes certain foods are misidentified as enemies. This can provoke an immune response so severe that bodily tissues swell and other symptoms of illness appear. The person is said to be allergic to that food and must avoid eating it.

There are many different kinds of allergies. Pollen is another harmless substance that triggers an unnecessary immune response in some people. The watering eyes and runny nose of hay fever are the result of the immune system's assault on what it has falsely labeled a dangerous enemy.

Many people are allergic to one or more of the foods shown in this photograph.

Allergy sufferers would be far better off if their immune systems could learn to ignore the pollen.

Anaphylactic shock is a dangerous kind of allergic reaction. It occurs when a person has a violent immune response to a normally harmless substance, such as shellfish, or a mildly harmful substance, such as bee venom. The massive swelling caused by the immune response may restrict or stop breathing or restrict blood flow. The condition can be fatal.

The immune system can also cause problems during transplant procedures. The immune system identifies the cells of a transplanted organ, such as a kidney or a heart, or of transplanted tissue, such as skin or bone, as foreign. For many years, transplants were difficult because the body's immune system relentlessly attacked, or rejected, the new cells. Surgeons have found two ways to reduce organ rejection. First, they carefully match transplant recipients with donors so that the cells are as genetically similar as possible. Second, they inject the recipient with drugs that suppress, or partially turn off, the immune system so it does not attack the transplanted tissue.

The most serious malfunctions of the immune system are *autoimmune reactions.* In an autoimmune reaction, the immune system mistakes healthy body cells for foreign invaders and unleashes its potent arsenal of weapons against them. Medical research suggests that multiple sclerosis is a kind of autoimmune reaction. Some of the evidence for this follows:

- Medical researchers who purposely provoked an autoimmune reaction in rabbits found that the rabbits developed patches in their central nervous system similar to those found in MS patients.
- Scientists have produced antibodies that will attack myelin.
- Scientists have found that, under test conditions, the cells of people with MS produce an autoimmune response more often than the cells of people without MS.

• One of the more common indicators of MS is an increase in the level of certain antibodies in the spinal fluid.

In people with MS, the innocent victim of the immune system's attack is the myelin insulation found along nerve cells of the brain, spinal cord, and optic nerves. For some reason, the body's immune system mistakes the myelin for a dangerous antigen. As a result, white blood cells attack the myelin, and the immune system triggers the release of chemicals that cause the area around the myelin to swell. Eventually, the myelin sheath becomes frayed.

Without proper insulation, the electrical connections among groups of cells along the central nervous system become inefficient and unreliable. While afflicted nerves can often transmit some messages without much problem, other messages become garbled or are interrupted altogether. When a muscle does not receive a complete message from the brain, it may respond in unexpected ways.

The damage from an autoimmune attack on myelin may not be permanent or irreversible. Frequently, the body can repair the myelin. In addition, nerve fibers can adapt somewhat to improve faulty transmission of electric impulses. As a result, a person in the early stages of MS usually finds that the symptoms go away after a short time.

Even when myelin is repaired or nerve fibers adapt to myelin damage, the nervous system rarely functions as well as before the person developed the disease. Just as a person's skin may retain permanent scars after healing from a deep wound, a person's myelin may be left with scars after it is repaired. Scarred myelin does not transport messages as efficiently as healthy myelin.

Meanwhile, the immune system continues to mistake the myelin for a dangerous invader and launches further attacks. Eventually, myelin may become permanently scarred. If the damage covers a large enough area, nerve communication may be disrupted. These scars are the plaques that are visible in magnetic resonance imaging studies.

Although most medical experts now believe that MS is an autoimmune disease, there is still no positive proof of this. A few researchers continue to look for other possible causes.

Chapter Three

THE SYMPTOMS OF MULTIPLE SCLEROSIS

As Annette Funicello discovered, MS is a particularly unsettling disease because experts offer only a vague idea of what people who contract it can expect. The term "multiple" in multiple sclerosis refers not only to the number of plaques, but also to the number, variety, and severity of problems that MS can bring.

MS is unpredictable because the nervous system is so complex and because the damage caused by immune system attacks can be so varied.

- Damage to myelin may be permanent, or it may be temporary.

- Some MS plaques are less than a millimeter in diameter, while others are more than 1 inch (2.5 centimeters) across. Larger patches do not always affect more areas of nerve communication.
- Symptoms vary considerably, depending on how much of the nervous system is affected and what type of nerve messages the plaques interrupt.
- Plaques that disrupt nerve connections several feet in length do not necessarily produce more noticeable symptoms than those that disrupt nerve connections only a fraction of an inch long.
- A single, small patch of destroyed myelin may be located at a crucial point where several nerve pathways intersect and, thus, cause a number of severe problems. On the other hand, a larger patch located in an anatomically less crucial area of the nervous system may cause only a single, barely noticeable symptom.

Not only are people with MS at a loss as to what symptoms to expect, they also have no way of knowing how, or even whether, the disease will progress. Again, the kind of MS a person develops depends on which nervous-system pathways are interrupted by damaged myelin and how severe the damage is.

Some people with MS experience only a few mild symptoms. These symptoms may appear only once and never return, or they may never grow serious enough to cause problems. Autopsies have found MS plaques in people who never displayed any symptoms of the disease during their lives. This *benign* form of the disease occurs in about 20 percent of those with MS.

By contrast, others experience problems that gradually grow worse throughout their lives. This is called *primary progressive multiple sclerosis*. It occurs in 10 to 20 percent of those with the disease.

Another group experiences a roller-coaster ride of relapses. In these cases, problems can appear rather suddenly. Each *flare-up* is a sign that the body's immune system has attacked and destroyed myelin. For the 20 to 30 percent of people with *relapsing-remitting multiple sclerosis*, the symptoms gradually improve after the initial onslaught. Then, weeks, months, or even years later, similar or different problems appear and fade away. There is no way of predicting when or how often these flare-ups and remissions will occur. Sometimes the symptoms disappear entirely during remissions. But, as Brian Apatoff, director of the Multiple Sclerosis Clinical Care and Research Center at New York Hospital observes, "You may never come back to your baseline if there is permanent damage to the brain or the spinal cord."[6]

The most common form of MS, which occurs in about 40 percent of the total cases, is known as *relapsing-progressive multiple sclerosis*. For these people, the unpredictable attacks gradually produce more severe symptoms.

Even for people within the same MS category, symptoms can vary dramatically. However, some general statements can be made about MS:

- MS is not a fatal disease. People have died of symptoms related to MS, but the fact that the nerve connections are interrupted is not, by itself, life threatening.
- MS is not contagious. A person who has the disease cannot pass it to someone else through bacteria or viruses.
- Although flare-ups may appear without warning, and a flare-up may have serious neurologic consequences, MS generally progresses slowly. Symptoms gradually become more severe over many years.
- Nine out of ten people with MS experience long stretches of time with few or no symptoms. In many cases, the symptoms of the first attack of MS

disappear within a month or so and do not recur for quite some time. In other cases, problems may wax and wane. If a person with MS experiences continuous problems that do not go away, he or she probably has the primary progressive form of the disease.

The individual symptoms that a person with MS will experience are impossible to predict and depend on the location of inflammation in the brain or spinal cord. They may include:

- difficulty with balance and coordination because myelin damage interrupts or distorts messages to various muscles
- facial pain
- muscle weakness
- constant fatigue or relentless generalized pain and achiness
- difficulty performing routine tasks with their hands or fingers
- trouble getting up from a sitting position or problems walking—from a slight unsteadiness and weakness to a total inability to stand

Over the years, walking difficulties associated with MS have been overemphasized. As a result, many people think of MS as a crippling disease that automatically robs a person of the ability to walk. This misconception was reinforced in early fund-raising appeals that almost always showed people with MS in wheelchairs and referred to the disease as "The Crippler of Young Adults." In reality, at least two-thirds of those with MS are still able to walk even after 25 years with the disease. A strong majority of individuals with MS remain active and independent.

Because the central nervous system controls the movement of such a variety of muscles, MS can also cause diverse problems ranging from a lack of bladder and bowel control to slurred speech. Besides difficulties associated with muscles, many common symptoms of MS are related to the senses. Many individuals with MS feel a numbness in the limbs or a change in their sensitivity to touch. The disease frequently affects the eyes, causing blurred or double vision, dizziness, blind spots, or even temporary blindness. These problems can appear without warning.

Multiple sclerosis often strikes people between the ages of 20 and 40. This woman's MS is so severe that she must use a wheelchair.

Chapter Four

WHO GETS MULTIPLE SCLEROSIS?

Multiple sclerosis is primarily a disease that strikes people between 20 and 40 years old. It is an especially expensive disease because it waylays people when they are most productive in terms of working and earning money. A survey conducted in the 1980s found that more than 75 percent of Americans, Australians, and Britains with MS were unemployed. A more recent survey found that 40 percent of individuals with MS leave the workforce, while 10 percent change occupations. Estimates concerning the economic effects of MS vary wildly, but most agree that the United

States alone spends more than $1 billion annually in medical treatment, social services, lost wages, and work missed.

More than 1 million people in the world have MS at any one time. The United States has a relatively high rate of MS patients compared to most of the world. Roughly 1 percent of the U.S. population—approximately 250,000 to 350,000 people—has been diagnosed with MS. Most experts believe the actual number of cases is at least one-third higher. Many cases go unreported because it is difficult to diagnose MS and because those with very minor symptoms may go untreated.

Interestingly, MS is most common in cooler regions of the world. Cases of MS are rare in the tropics and subtropics. In the United States, most cases occur above a latitude of 37° north and in Europe above 45° north. Residents of the northern United States are nearly three times more likely to get MS as those who live in the southern states, while the United States's northern neighbor, Canada, has an MS rate nearly double that of the United States.

Location is not the only factor that influences whether a person is likely to develop MS. Ethnic background appears to play a significant role. MS is a disease of northern Europeans and their descendants. Asians rarely develop MS. Even in Seattle, Washington, which has a higher than average rate of MS, the rate among residents of Japanese background is lower than average. Inuit and African populations are also largely MS-free.

Studies have found that some people carry their susceptibility to MS wherever they go. Immigrants often experience MS at the same rate as people in their native country, rather than at the rate of people in their new country.

More than twice as many women as men develop MS. Men, however, are more likely to develop primary progressive MS than women. Women tend to display symptoms of MS earlier than men. On average, women develop their first symptoms at age 25, while men do not show signs of the disease until age 28.

MS has a slight tendency to run in families. Children of a parent who has MS are fifteen to twenty times more likely than the rest of the population to get MS.

Infection or Faulty Genes?

The statistics detailing who gets MS have provided an intriguing and baffling set of clues about what causes a person's immune system to mistakenly attack myelin and, as a result, cause MS. Some of the clues point to a bacteria or virus being the culprit.

During the 1964 Winter Olympics, Jimmy Heuga of the United States and Egon Zimmerman and Josef Steigler, both Austrians, all won medals in the alpine skiing competition. Surprisingly, all three eventually developed multiple sclerosis. The odds of MS striking three friends and competitors in a single event are incredibly small. Could something in the

Jim Heuga navigating a tight turn during the 1964 Winter Olympics

environment, such as a bacteria or virus, have triggered the disease in all three men?

More conventional laboratory evidence for the involvement of a virus comes from animal studies showing that viruses can cause relapses in MS patients. Anything that can trigger a relapse should be viewed as a possible cause of the original disease. Also, laboratory analyses of MS patients show that they often have abnormal levels of viral antibodies. These antibodies would be manufactured only in response to a viral infection.

How could a virus or bacteria cause the human immune system to attack itself? Perhaps T-cells are somehow tricked into attacking the wrong cells. Perhaps the surface markers of the enemy antigens closely resemble those of myelin. If so, the immune system might produce antibodies that would attack myelin that has been mistakenly identified as an antigen. This type of reaction is known as a cross-reaction.

Scientists have firmly established the existence of cross-reactions, and have used it in creating vaccines. By injecting a person with a relatively harmless organism that is similar to a harmful one, doctors can provoke the immune system to produce antibodies that react against the harmful organism. These antibodies can provide the person with immunity against a deadly disease, should it ever invade his or her body.

The arguments in favor of a bacteria or virus triggering MS run into problems, however. If something in the environment causes MS, why do immigrants develop MS at the same rate as people in their native country? If a person moves from an area where MS is common to an area where it is rare, shouldn't he or she be less likely to develop MS than a person who remains in the high-risk area?

Many experts argue for a different kind of trigger. They believe that malfunctioning genes bring about MS. George Ebers, a physician at the University of Western Ontario, Canada, performed a study in the mid-1990s that shed some light on this subject. He was intrigued when one of his MS patients told him that the daughter she had given up for adoption more than 30 years earlier had also developed the disease. The two did not share the same environment, but they did share the same genes. This story seemed to indicate that the increased incidence of MS among members of the same family was the result of genetic similarities, not a virus that had been passed within a household.

Ebers then tracked the rate at which adopted children of individuals with MS developed the disease. He found that the adopted children had the same risk of developing MS as the general population. On the other hand, children born to individuals with MS are fifteen to twenty times more likely to get MS than the general population. "The increased risk seems entirely attributable to genes," concluded Ebers.[7]

Studies of twins have supported the idea that genetics, and not something in the immediate environment, leads to the development of MS. A 1986 report in the *New England Journal of Medicine* compared the incidence of MS in identical twins

George Ebers treats patients with MS at the University of Western Ontario in Canada.

(those who share the same genes) with the rate in fraternal twins (those who share the same parents, but do not share an identical set of genes). The study found that when one fraternal twin has MS, the other twin has the same chance of developing MS as any other family member (3 to 5 percent). But when one identical twin has MS, the other twin has a greater than 25 percent chance of developing the disease.

Furthermore, the spouse of an individual with MS is no more likely than members of the general population to get the disease. All of this evidence points to something in a person's genetic makeup as the cause of MS.

Renegade Cells

How could genes cause an immune system to attack the wrong substances? Some immunologists have proposed that virtually all immune systems accidentally produce a few T-cells that cannot distinguish myelin from foreign cells. In most people, these *renegade T-cells* are kept under control by a self-policing immune mechanism. However, if something goes wrong with that mechanism, the renegade T-cells may multiply until there are enough of them to cause a problem.

When the unruly T-cells cause enough damage, the immune system eventually takes action. It reacts quickly and harshly to shut the T-cells down. Such a reaction would explain the relapsing and remitting nature of MS. Symptoms appear only when renegade T-cells are too numerous. Once the immune system's defenses respond, the symptoms go away until the next buildup of renegade T-cells.

Phillipa Marrack and John Kappler, a husband-and-wife immune research team working in Denver, Colorado, have actually found evidence of renegade T-cells and a corresponding regulating mechanism. They discovered that many T-cells cannot differentiate between "self" molecules and foreign molecules.

Marrack and Kappler identified and studied one type of T-cell in mice. They found that some of the cells showed signs of attacking the mice tissue, but only a few of them ever left the thymus (where they were produced). Apparently, the mice had some sort of regulatory mechanism that eliminated dangerous, self-attacking cells.

These results led Marrack to conclude that humans may well have immune cells that react to our own body. She believes that the immune system purges most of these faulty T-cells before they are mature. The few renegade T-cells that do reach maturity and leave the thymus are generally too weak to cause any real problems. If Marrack's theory is correct, MS could develop when a person's immune regulatory mechanism fails to keep these cells in check.

Other researchers suggest that the immune-system mechanism responsible for teaching T-cells to recognize self molecules may be to blame. A specific group of genes, known as the *major histocompatibility complex* (MHC), holds the key to the body's recognition of self molecules. These genes instruct cells to make MHC proteins, which become surface markers on cells. In essence, these surface markers are "free passes," permitting cells to remain in the body with no danger of attack from the immune system. When B-cells display an antigen on their surface for examination by T-cells, the B-cells also display a MHC protein, as if offering a comparison between a safe molecule and a suspicious intruder.

Diane Faustman of the Harvard Medical School in Boston, Massachusetts, has conducted experiments showing that the number of MHC proteins is greatly reduced in people with diabetes, which, like MS, is an autoimmune disease. If these MHC proteins are absent or not working properly, the T-cells may have trouble identifying the molecules they challenge. In that case, they could easily mistake body tissues for foreign antigens.

Researchers have gathered other clues that genetics plays a role in the development of autoimmune diseases. The autoimmune disease rheumatoid arthritis is more likely to develop in people with a specific gene than in people without that gene. Scientists have also found several genetic markers, or segments of genes, that, when present in a person's DNA (deoxyribonucleic acid), indicate a greater than normal chance of acquiring Type I diabetes.

Despite the evidence of genetic involvement in autoimmune diseases, genetics does not entirely explain the appearance of MS. Many people who develop MS have no history of the disease in their family. Furthermore, only a small minority of the people who have genes associated with autoimmune diseases develop MS. These facts suggest that defective genes are only part of the story.

The current opinion in the medical community is that genetic factors make a person more or less vulnerable to MS. Most experts believe that something else is responsible for setting the disease in motion. Once this trigger upsets the immune system, the disease develops. The question that continues to baffle researchers is: What might that trigger be?

The Mysterious Trigger

Although immunologists have made great strides in understanding the workings of the body's defense system, they are nowhere near finding the "smoking gun"—the evidence that would reveal what triggers the immune system to attack the body it is designed to protect.

It may be that the conflicting evidence about infectious agents and genetic factors means that both are involved in producing MS. Perhaps a bacteria or virus triggers MS in people who are genetically susceptible to the disease. Autoimmune diseases do frequently appear in people who have recently had an infection, although this has not been established in the case of MS. Children with rheumatoid arthritis often show signs of bacterial or viral infection just before the disease appears. In 1991, German and American researchers working with rats found that *Yersinia enterocolitica*, a bacteria that causes an infection of the digestive tract, can initiate a thyroid disease similar to an autoimmune disease called Graves' disease.

Marrack has developed a scenario that would explain how bacteria and viruses might trigger a host of autoimmune diseases; including MS. She suggests that certain antigens, called superantigens, may be capable of confusing the immune system. A normal antigen fits only into the T-cell receptor designed to recognize it. But a superantigen acts like a master key—it can open up many T-cell receptors.

As a result, the immune system detects the presence of a harmful invader, but is so confused by the antigen's surface marker that it cannot figure out exactly what the invader is. Instead of destroying the superantigen by producing one specific antibody that works against it, the immune system unleashes a wild, blind barrage of immune activity in an effort to knock out the invader. This is something like randomly dropping hundreds of bombs over an area in the hope that one will hit the target.

This type of response is known to happen with certain bacteria, such as the staphylococci that cause food poisoning. These bacteria give off a toxin that triggers a response in many different kinds of T-cells. All these T-cells fire off chemical messages to their various B-cell counterparts as well as to other immune-system components. The result is a poisonous overdose of immune activity that makes the person extremely ill.

A superantigen may stimulate thousands of different types of T-cells. A number of immunologists, including Marrack, suggest that an autoimmune disease might be caused when a hyperactive immune reaction to a superantigen stimulates some of the normally ineffective, self-attacking T-cells. These renegade T-cells send messages to B-cells, causing them to crank out an army of self-attacking antibodies, or autoantibodies. The autoantibodies then spread through the body in search of the "enemy" they are supposed to attack. In the case of MS, the autoantibodies attack myelin.

In 1991, Marrack and Kappler demonstrated that superantigens can be produced by viruses as well as by bacteria. While the superantigen theory is intriguing, research into the

Phillipa Marack and John Kapplar conduct immunology research in Denver, Colorado.

causes of MS has not found a specific virus connected with the disease.

There is another reason that it is so difficult to pinpoint exactly what causes MS. Many experts believe that the disease may be triggered by an environmental factor that affects a person more than a decade before signs of MS ever appear—probably during childhood, near the age of puberty. A person may be susceptible to the trigger for only a few years. By the time the person begins to show symptoms of MS, the disease-causing factor is long gone. This scenario offers the best explanation for why people who immigrate after age 15 show the same rate of MS as those in their native country, rather than their new neighbors.

Because researchers still do not know how MS develops, they can make only three general statements about why certain people develop symptoms.

- It tends to develop in individuals who are susceptible as a result of genetic inheritance.
- It is probably triggered by exposure at an early age to something in the environment, such as a bacterium, a virus, a superantigen, a pollutant, radiation, or a toxin.
- Genetically related family members, people of northern European ancestry, and women have a greater risk than the general population of developing the disease.

Until the mystery of the MS trigger is revealed, there is no way to predict who will get the disease, nor is there any way to prevent it.

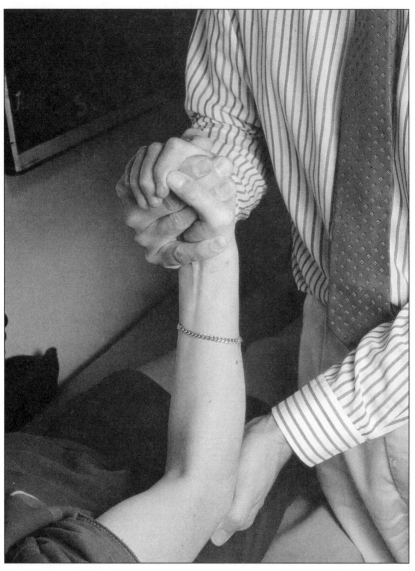

A doctor tests the reflexes of a person with multiple sclerosis.

Chapter Five

DIAGNOSING MULTIPLE SCLEROSIS

Multiple sclerosis casts a shadow of uncertainty and anxiety wherever it strikes. A century ago, the symptoms described by MS patients seemed so inexplicable that doctors often attributed them to psychiatric problems. Even today, the confusing array of symptoms, the unpredictability of the course of the disease, the wide range of disease severity, and the seemingly random breakdown of unrelated body parts make MS difficult to detect.

To make matters worse, none of the symptoms of the disease are unique to MS. Any symptoms that occur in MS, from numb limbs and unsteadiness in walking to blurred vision, are also characteristic of a number of other neurologic illnesses. Doctors need to eliminate a great number of possibilities, including tumors, strokes, and epilepsy, before settling on MS as the cause of the problems.

Because MS has no symptoms that distinguish it from other medical conditions, it is seldom detected until at least a year or two after the appearance of the first symptoms. In many cases, the diagnosis is not confirmed until 5 years after the first symptoms appear. This means an individual often must endure months, or even years, of tests and visits to doctors. In the meantime, patients live in limbo. The stress of not knowing what is wrong can take a tremendous toll. During their years of uncertainty, they may experience frustration and despair as the treatments that the doctors prescribe have little lasting effect.

Because many different parts of the body may be affected, patients are often shuffled among a variety of specialists. According to some estimates, the average MS patient sees eight doctors before the correct diagnosis made.

For many years, doctors had to rely on guesswork to diagnose MS. There was no method, short of an autopsy, for determining whether a person had the disease. Unfortunately, Jean-Martin Charcot muddied the waters even further when he classified only a few symptoms as being characteristic of MS. This led to incorrect diagnoses and confusion for nearly a century. Doctors did not know what to make of patients who showed symptoms besides the ones Charcot had identified.

Today, once physicians zero in on MS as a probable diagnosis, the testing process can often be concluded fairly quickly. Doctors can confirm, with 95 percent accuracy, whether or not a person has MS. But the decisive tests can be very expensive, and most doctors will not order them until they strongly suspect MS.

In 1869, Jean-Martin Charcot presented a paper describing three patients with multiple sclerosis to the French Biological Society.

Detecting Multiple Sclerosis

Why does MS take so long to diagnose? In many cases, the characteristics of the illness appear in a pattern that only gradually becomes apparent. Even if a doctor suspects MS, he or she must wait to see if characteristic MS patterns continue to appear.

For this reason, a patient's medical history is extremely important for diagnosing the disease. The doctor considers not only what the patient is experiencing but also what symptoms the patient displayed years earlier, in seemingly unrelated episodes. One red flag alerting physicians to the possibility of MS is difficulty with the senses, such as experiencing symptoms of numbness or blurred vision. If problems with the eyes or other senses, or with the muscles, crop up at odd intervals over a number of years, the physician will begin to suspect MS.

Physical examinations also play a role in the diagnosis. The eyes of individuals with MS often show an abnormal reflex response when light is shined in them. Hypersensitive muscle reflexes are another possible indicator of the disease. This sensitivity can be detected simply by hitting a joint, such as a knee, with a rubber hammer. The normal reflex response is a single contraction. A hypersensitive muscle may contract repeatedly to a single blow. Other possible indications of multiple sclerosis are abnormal muscle stiffness or weakness, awkward or uncoordinated movements, and difficulty walking due to weakness or poor balance.

Testing for Multiple Sclerosis

In the early stages of the diagnosis, physicians classify suspected MS patients as "possible" or "probable." To confirm a case as "definite," doctors need to be able to see what is happening inside the nervous system. Medical researchers have developed laboratory tests and a number of remarkable devices that make this possible. With these procedures, a physician may be able to make a diagnosis of MS within a week.

Some of these tests do not confirm the presence of MS but rather aid physicians by ruling out other diseases with similar symptoms. For example, an *electroencephalogram* (EEG) measures electrical activity in the brain. To conduct an EEG, electrodes are attached to the patient's scalp. The brain is then stimulated and the electrical responses recorded. MS does not have a measurable effect on the brain's electrical activity. An EEG is performed to rule out epilepsy, which can produce some symptoms that are similar to those of MS.

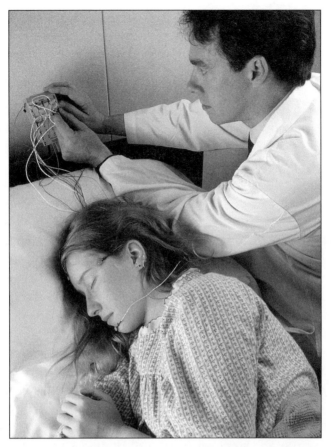

During an electroencephalogram (EEG), scientists stimulate and observe electrical activity in a person's brain.

Computerized tomography (CT) scans perform a similar service. During a CT scan, the patient lies flat on a table that slides partway into the CT machine. A scanner then rotates around the patient's head, shooting a narrow beam of X rays at each of the dozens of stops it makes during its rotation. Each burst of X rays produces a picture of a thin, cross-sectional slice of the brain. The images are compiled by a computer into a three-dimensional picture.

CT scans are valuable in detecting intracranial pathology such as strokes, hemorrhages, and lesions. However, they have limited use in detecting the demyelinization that occurs in people with MS.

A myelogram can detect compression of the spinal cord that may cause symptoms similar to those of MS. This test involves injecting dye into the spinal fluid and then taking an X-ray image. This procedure is seldom performed now that MRI technology is readily available.

Spinal taps are another common procedure used to help detect the presence of MS. Although the words "spinal tap" provoke shudders and winces from most people, this test is actually relatively quick and painless. Technicians withdraw a sample of spinal fluid, the liquid that surrounds the spinal cord and protects it by serving as a shock absorber. This liquid is then analyzed. Certain antibodies and myelin proteins are often found in the spinal fluid of people with MS. While this test can suggest the presence of MS, it cannot confirm the diagnosis. Other diseases can cause similar changes to the spinal fluid.

Today physicians use MRIs to confirm the diagnosis of MS. The technique, first demonstrated in 1946 by Edward Purcell and Felix Bloch of the United States, uses magnetic waves to analyze the composition of body tissues. Like the CT scan, patients are placed on a flat platform that slides into a large, hollow, metal cylinder. Instead of bombarding the patient with X rays, the MRI bounces radio waves off the person's body.

The metal cylinder surrounds the patient with a magnetic field. A computer charts the electromagnetic charges in the patient's brain by recording variations in the energy level of hydrogen atom nuclei of the brain cells during the radio-wave bombardment. The result is an exceptionally clear picture of the brain that can reveal subtle differences in tissue. That is why a MRI is very good at detecting the numerous scattered plaques associated with MS.

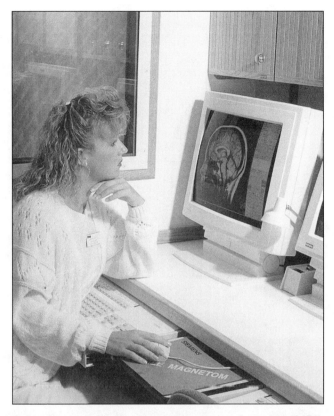

Scientists can use magnetic resonance imaging (MRI) to look at a person's brain tissue. It is the only way to determine whether a person has MS.

The MRI is an extremely expensive test, and it is not fool-proof. A MRI of the brain may not pick up on MS plaques in the first few months of the disease, and it will not detect plaques confined to the spinal cord.

A healthy lifestyle that includes eating plenty of fruits and vegetables is important for people with MS.

Chapter Six

TREATING MULTIPLE SCLEROSIS

There is presently no cure for MS, nor is one likely to be developed until the cause of the disease is discovered. Nevertheless, there are many things individuals with MS can do to reduce its negative effects and to prevent their symptoms from worsening. A healthy lifestyle is especially important. Infections and injuries can cause MS flare-ups. Therefore, exercising regularly, getting enough sleep, and eating healthfully are all important for MS patients.

Experiments also show that the use of alcohol and tobacco can inhibit the immune system and place extra burdens on the nervous system. They are also associated with many preventable diseases of the heart, lungs, and liver. Although it is wise to avoid tobacco and minimize use of alcohol, these substances are not known to be specifically detrimental to people with MS.

Stress has been shown to cause changes in the immune system. Prolonged periods of stress can intensify certain symptoms of MS such as fatigue, pain, and nervousness. It is doubtful that stress actually causes flare-ups of MS.

People with MS must steer a path between inactivity and overwork. Exercise is important for maintaining health and fitness. Physical therapy may help people retrain muscles that have been affected by their disease. It may also improve stamina and endurance. Yet exhaustion has been shown to intensify MS symptoms. Those with MS must learn to exercise sensibly and to know their limits. This is especially true during flare-ups. When symptoms develop, the best thing a person with MS can do is get plenty of rest and avoid too much physical activity until the flare-up subsides.

Sixty years ago, many doctors prescribed heat as a treatment for MS. In fact, they often recommended that patients move to a warmer climate. Research has since shown that nerves do not transmit messages well at high temperatures. Since the basic problem with MS is inefficient transmission of nervous-system messages, people with MS are better off in cool climates. They should also avoid hot lights, heating pads, and hot tubs.

Individuals with MS can live more comfortably if they make lifestyle changes to accommodate their situation. Depending on the particular symptoms, these changes may include using a cane, a walker, or a wheelchair; making their home wheelchair-accessible; living in a one-story home to avoid stairs; installing grab bars in hallways and in bathrooms; and replacing twist handles on faucets with lever handles.

For some young adults, a diagnosis of MS can affect decisions about careers and whether or not to have children. MS has no physical effect on the ability of a couple to have chil-

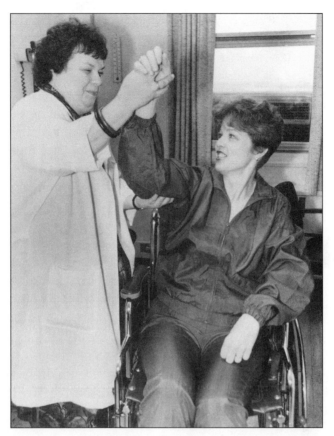

A nurse helps a patient with MS lift her arm during a physical therapy session at the Albert Einstein College of Medicine in the Bronx, New York.

dren. Pregnancy has no harmful effects on people with MS; in fact, symptoms often improve during pregnancy. However, prospective parents must consider their physical ability to care for a child. The unpredictability of MS makes such decisions all the more difficult.

Psychological and Emotional Treatment

Uncertainty about the course that MS will take and frustration over the symptoms can cause emotional and psychological stress. Depression, anxiety, and anger are normal responses to such a situation. But if left unresolved, these reactions can make it difficult to maintain relationships with spouses, children, coworkers, and friends.

People with MS can better manage these emotional and psychological effects by facing facts early and learning as much as possible about the disease. Friends and family can help by being patient and allowing the person to vent feelings of frustration and anger. MS support groups and therapists experienced in working with MS patients can provide emotional support, guidance, and practical assistance. Employers can help by adapting work conditions to fit the person's needs.

As is true for people with any disease, those with MS cope better by maintaining as much independence as they can without overdoing it. This means getting the essential help without leaning too heavily on those around them. Medical problems are better taken to doctors than left to spouses. Children should be encouraged to help when appropriate, but parents with MS must not overburden their children with adult responsibilities. Health experts advise patients to "take MS out of relationships," that is, to deal with people person-to-person rather than person-to-person-with-MS.

Phony Treatments

The unpredictable nature of MS and the frustration and anxiety it causes can make MS patients easy targets for useless treatments. When someone suffers a severe attack of symptoms, takes a prescribed treatment, and then watches the symptoms miraculously disappear, he or she may believe that the treatment worked. Yet with MS, after the first appearance of symptoms most people experience complete recovery. Flare-ups usually fade away in a few weeks without any treatment. This pattern can make it appear that a treatment used during that time worked and can lead to many dubious claims of miracle cures.

Furthermore, there are documented cases in which MS has disappeared without any apparent reason. Entertainer Lola

Falana had MS for a number of years before one day waking up and finding that her symptoms had disappeared—never to return. "I've heard it attributed to everything from prayer to ski-jumping," Annette Funicello says.[8] When someone tries a new treatment and then experiences such a recovery, he or she is likely to enthusiastically proclaim it a miracle cure.

The desperation of MS patients, combined with the hope offered by cases of MS remission or disappearance, has produced a large number of bizarre "cures." The treatments range from cobra venom and special diets to electric shock. Some advocates of these treatments are well intentioned; others are out-and-out frauds.

Desperation can cloud the reasoning of even the most intelligent, rational people. Ellen Burstyn MacFarlane was a news reporter who specialized in rooting out cases of consumer fraud. She knew all the tricks of those who prey on human hopes and fears. MacFarlane also had MS.

In 1991, MacFarlane read a cover story in *New York* magazine about a wonderful new medical treatment called "Superesonant Wavenergy." The article detailed how Dr. Irving Dardik's new technique of abruptly raising and lowering a patient's heart rate through carefully monitored exercise was achieving spectacular results. Dardik explained that the procedure corrected internal imbalances that caused diseases such as MS.

Hopeful that this was the medical breakthrough for which she had been longing, MacFarlane approached Dardik. The doctor assured her that he could not merely improve her condition but could actually cure it. The process, however, would be expensive. Dardik charged her $100,000 for a year of treatment. In addition, MacFarlane had to purchase expensive exercise machines and computer equipment to monitor her heart rate.

As experienced as she was at spotting consumer deception, MacFarlane went ahead with the program. In the first 2 months, the rigorous one-on-one exercise program with Dardik showed encouraging results. MacFarlane saw noticeable

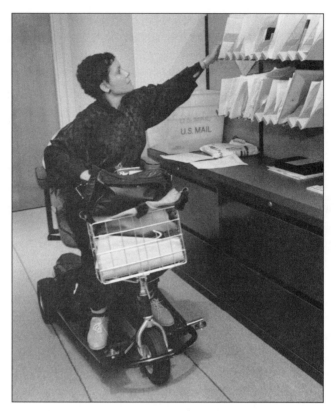

Ellen Burstyn MacFarlane at work

gains in strength and her energy level rose. By January 1992, she was able to walk the length of her house without assistance—something she had not been able to do for a long time. The cure seemed worth the staggering price.

But almost as suddenly as it started work, the cure began to fail. MacFarlane deteriorated so badly that by March she could barely move. Dardik continued to assure her that she was on the road to recovery despite the temporary setback. But he began to pay less and less attention to her. By May, MacFarlane was so weak that she could no longer dress herself or even use the bathroom without assistance. Only after paying a fortune and suffering through 11 months of false hope, did MacFarlane finally admit that she had been duped. Her only consolation was that, after bringing charges against Dardik, she was able to drive him out of business.

MS experts stress that there is no diet, exercise, precaution, vitamin program, or mechanical device that has proven effective in the treatment of MS. Patients should be especially leery of any claims that a particular treatment can "cure" MS. The National Multiple Sclerosis Society funds more research and provides more programs for people with MS and their families than any other voluntary health agency in the world. It examines claims of beneficial treatments and alerts the public to scams and phony treatments.

Medical Treatments

Although the medical world has made occasional breakthroughs in the treatment of autoimmune diseases over the years, little progress has been made in finding preventative strategies, cures, or effective treatments for multiple sclerosis. Researchers have been thwarted by their inability to pin down the cause of the disease and by the complex mysteries of the immune system.

As a result, medical treatment for MS has focused on helping patients get through flare-ups. Doctors have prescribed drugs known as *corticosteroids* to help reduce swelling. Long-term treatment with corticosteroids, such as methylprednisolone, suppresses the immune system's production of antibodies so there are fewer of them to attack the myelin.

Unfortunately, steroids do not target a particular antibody. While slowing down the antibodies' attack on myelin, steroids also attack the rest of the immune system. This can lead to unpleasant and even harmful side effects, and the weakened immune system leaves the body vulnerable to invaders. Steroids must be rationed carefully. Although they can be useful in the short term for reducing swelling in an MS relapse, they have no long-term effect on the severity or frequency of future relapses.

Other common treatments for symptoms include antibiotics to cure infections that might trigger flare-ups, medication and acupuncture to relieve pain, drugs that reduce stiffness in the muscles, and medication to regulate bladder and bowel control.

Recently, the treatment of MS has undergone radical changes. In the past few years, researchers have developed new treatment regimens that do more than just alleviate the symptoms of flare-ups. They actually slow the progression of the disease. These new treatments include interferon therapy, myelin decoys, and a variety of drugs that selectively suppress specific parts of the immune system.

On July 23, 1993, the U.S. Food and Drug Administration (FDA) approved the use of *interferon* beta-1b, the first drug that has proven effective in reducing the frequency and severity of MS flare-ups. Interferons are a family of proteins discovered in the early 1970s. They are produced naturally in the human body by certain T-cells during times of infection. Although no one knows exactly how interferon works, it appears to have some role in regulating the immune system. One of its effects is to suppress certain autoimmune responses.

Tests conducted with Betaseron, a form of a genetically engineered interferon beta-1b, show that it is effective in reducing both the severity and the frequency of MS flare-ups. In one experiment, individuals treated with Betaseron had an average of 2.7 attacks over 3 years. Those given a placebo (a treatment with no active ingredients) experienced an average of four relapses during the same period of time.

In another study, Ludwig Kappos of the University Hospital in Basel, Switzerland, evaluated the effects of interferon beta-1b (Betaseron) on 700 people with progressive MS. After a 3-year trial, Kappos concluded that the drug slowed the deterioration of nerve functions. This was the first time any drug had been shown to help to people with this form of MS.

Following FDA approval, demand for the drug was so high that manufacturers could not produce enough to go around. The medication had to be distributed by lottery.

In the spring of 1996, a second interferon product, interferon beta-1a, was approved for market by the FDA. So far, the treatment, which is sold under the name Avonex, has shown promising results. In a study completed in 1998, a team of researchers treated more than 500 people with relapsing-remitting MS over a 2-year period. They divided the patients into three groups. One group received a high dose of inter feron beta-1a, the second group received a low dose of interferon beta-1a, and a third group received a placebo. According to study leader George Ebers, the high-dose group experienced a 33 percent fewer relapses than the control group. The low-dose group had 27 percent fewer relapses than the control group. The interferon product also appeared to slow the advance of disabling symptoms.

Beta interferon treatments are expensive, costing between $7,000 and $12,000 for a year's supply. The drug must be self-injected by the patient. Betaseron must be injected every other day, while Avonex must be injected once a week. Unfortunately, like many drugs, Betaseron and Avonex have unpleasant side effects. The most uncomfortable side effects include flulike symptoms and irritation of the skin.

One of the more promising lines of research involves the development of substances that mimic myelin. Ruth Arnon, Michael Sela, and Dvora Teitelbaum have spent more than two decades working on this approach at the Weizmann Institute of Science in Israel. They successfully created a synthetic replica of a protein contained in human myelin cells. When they injected the synthetic glatiramor acetate protein into guinea pigs, it triggered an immune-system reaction similar to that which occurs against myelin in individuals with MS. But while the immune system reacted against the myelin look-alike, it did not launch a similar attack against the actual myelin.

The researchers hope that this artificial protein will act as a decoy, coaxing the immune system into attacking it instead of the myelin. Sela sees this as a possible "synthetic vaccine against

Ruth Arnon (left), Michael Sela (center), and Dvora Teitelbaum (right) conduct scientific research at the Weizmann Institute of Science in Rehovot, Israel.

multiple sclerosis."[9] In 1997, the FDA approved the sale of Copaxone, which is a form of glatiramor acetate.

The advantage of Copaxone is that it does not cause flu-like side effects. The disadvantage is that it requires daily injections. Its side effects may include tightness in the chest and heart palpitations. Experts caution users not to expect dramatic results from these drugs. Neither Copaxone nor beta interferon treatments are cures, and they do not always produce noticeable results. "For a year or two, the drugs don't make them feel better. But I've had patients on Betaseron for 5 or 6 years, and you couldn't get them off with pliers," says Dr. Stanley van den Noort, chief medical officer of the National Multiple Sclerosis Society.[10]

Recent studies have shown that even during remissions, MS may destroy more than just myelin. The disease may eat away at the nerves themselves. As a result, many experts are now recommending that people with MS begin taking Avonex, Betaseron, or Copaxone as soon as they are diagnosed. Beginning treatment early may help prevent irreparable nerve damage.

Although the immune system is complex, scientists are beginning to find treatments that can alter one part of the immune system while leaving the rest intact. For example, cyclosporine is a substance that targets only T-helper cells—the T-cells that help speed up the production of antibodies. The drug has shown some promise in suppressing these cells while leaving the rest of the immune system alone.

In tests conducted at the University of Pittsburgh, a drug called FK 506 has shown some ability to suppress autoimmune reactions in patients with rheumatoid arthritis. Studies performed at the University of Florida have shown that a drug called azathioprine has the potential to prevent the autoimmune disease diabetes. As yet, however, neither drug has been effective in treating MS.

Another promising new drug goes by the unwieldy name of CTLA41g. This substance shuts off the immune response by interrupting the communications between T-cells and antigen-presenting cells. In experiments done on mice, the drug suppressed the production of antibodies. While its effect on the immune system does not last long, CTLA41g may be a powerful weapon in fighting autoimmune disease. It can work selectively against a particular immune response instead of shutting down the entire immune system. Several years of additional testing will be required before researchers can try this drug on humans.

Medical researchers have been moving forward on another front in their search for a selective weapon that will not shut down the whole immune system. This effort began in 1911 with a man named H. Gideon Wells. He performed experiments with guinea pigs suffering from anaphylactic shock, the immune system overreaction discussed in Chapter 2. He induced the reaction by injecting guinea pigs with a foreign protein. As a curious byproduct of his experimentation, Wells found that he could prevent the anaphylactic shock if he fed the animals that same protein for several weeks before the injection. Wells could not explain these results.

His discovery opened up a fascinating new pathway for researchers. They began experimenting with feeding antigens to animals with autoimmune diseases. Scientists first injected rats with a form of the myelin protein, causing them to develop an MS-like disease. When the rats were later fed myelin protein, they were dramatically cured.

The experiments showed that taking the antigen orally, so that it goes directly to the stomach, seems to build the body's tolerance to the substance. The treatment became known as *oral tolerization.* Although it is still unclear how oral tolerization works, scientists speculate that the proteins may stop the T-cells from sending messages.

The early research with oral tolerization in humans has shown great promise for treating MS. Many patients were able to reduce or completely eliminate the immune-suppressing drugs they had been taking to control their disease.

If the research continues to hold up, doctors may be on to an extremely valuable disease-fighting tool. This method of immune suppression is very selective; it blocks only the immune response against the proteins that are ingested. Since any given antigen provokes a response from only a few T-cells out of a million, the method leaves the overwhelming majority of the immune system intact.

The immune system's selective reaction to the ingested proteins leads researchers to believe that they can create a vaccine that would work against T-cells. If MS is indeed caused by T-cells that misidentify antigens, immunologists may be able to thwart the disease by fine-tuning a vaccine that protects the human body from renegade T-cells.

A variation on the vaccine approach involves engineering antibodies that will attack only selected renegade T-cells. Preliminary tests with MS patients given a dose of these antibodies have been encouraging. According to Hubert J. P. Schoemaker, who heads Centecor, Inc., a biotechnology company in Malvern, Pennsylvania, the technique could be "a major breakthrough if the effect continues to be found in large trials." [11]

Another high-tech approach in the fight against MS involves tying up the harmful T-cells with harmless molecules. Copies of the surface-marker molecules that will stimulate a T-cell attack are injected into the patient. The molecules latch onto the T-cells and prevent them from attacking the body's cells.

Some researchers believe that it is not faulty T-cells but rather faulty MHC proteins (the surface markers that identify self molecules as safe) that cause the symptoms of autoimmune diseases. If that is true, then scientists may find a cure for MS in genetic engineering. Perhaps new genes could be inserted to repair or reprogram the faulty MHC genes.

This solution will become more of a possibility when the Human Genome Project has been completed. The goal of this international research effort is to isolate and catalog the estimated 100,000 genes that direct a person's chemical makeup. This knowledge would also make it possible for scientists to compare the DNA of people with and without MS and note any differences. If researchers can isolate the precise genetic markers that indicate who is at risk for MS, they might be able to stop the disease before it starts.

Yet another avenue of MS research focuses on replacing myelin around damaged nerve fibers. This work is important because treatments aimed at stopping MS do very little to repair damage that has already occurred. Ian Duncan of the University of Wisconsin School of Veterinary Medicine recently transplanted myelin-producing cells into dogs with a disease that is similar to relapsing-progressive MS. The result was significant growth of myelin around the damaged nerve fibers. Previously, scientists did not think it was possible to regenerate myelin.

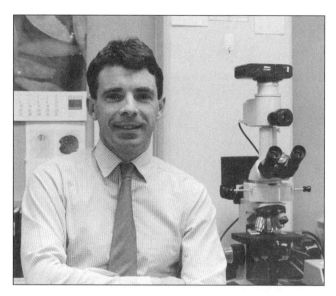

Ian Duncan is searching for ways to regenerate the myelin sheath that surrounds nerve fibers. He works at the University of Wisconsin School of Veterinary Medicine.

Finally, although most medical experts regard multiple sclerosis as an autoimmune disease, a few researchers continue to probe the possibility that something else, perhaps a disease of the myelin-producing cells, causes MS.

Hope for the Future

The complexity of the immune system and the uncertainties surrounding the cause of MS mean that researchers have their work cut out for them in finding a way to prevent or cure for the disease. Furthermore, the genetic engineering required for many treatments now being studied can be enormously expensive, and the treatments that result may not prove to be worth the cost.

Nevertheless, medical experts remain optimistic. Researchers have been able to stop the self-destruction of myelin in laboratory animals. A Stanford University research team working with mice has been able to cure a disease similar to

MS. One fortunate circumstance is that methods developed to treat any autoimmune disease can probably be adapted to MS. The rapid rate at which scientists are closing in on the secrets of the immune system offers encouragement to MS patients. Richard Lechtenberg, author of *The Multiple Sclerosis Fact Book,* echoes the optimism of many experts when he writes that "the discovery of both the cause of MS and its cure are probably not far in the future."[12]

Chapter Seven

LIVING WITH MULTIPLE SCLEROSIS

As Annette Funicello observed, it makes no sense for people with MS to sit around and wait for the cure that will make all their troubles magically disappear. For these people, MS and its symptoms are a fact of life now and for the foreseeable future.

Many people with MS have learned important lessons about dealing with the blessings and hardships of life. Their lives and their courage are a testimony to the strength of the human spirit. "I don't waste energy crying about 'what ifs,'" says Ellen Burstyn MacFarlane. "Instead, I am learning how to live with what is. For every bad moment, I have three good ones."[13] Such people often find that their courage brings out the best in others. A teacher in the Midwest, for example, found her students fighting over the privilege of pushing her wheelchair.

While medical and scientific explanations can provide a background for what occurs in cases of MS, the effects of the disease and the way people cope with them are best seen in the lives of those who face the disease every day. This chapter briefly tells the stories of some well-known people with MS. The disease affects each one in different ways, and each has reacted in his or her own way. Most of the stories describe seriously affected people simply because those with milder cases of MS often do not reveal their illness and generally have lifestyles that require little, if any, adjustments.

Bringing the Oklahoma City Bomber to Justice

On April 19, 1995, Joseph Hartzler was driving through his hometown of Springfield, Illinois, when he heard a horrifying news bulletin over the car radio. A gigantic bomb had exploded in downtown Oklahoma City, Oklahoma, shattering the Alfred P. Murrah federal building. As details of the tragedy emerged, the body count rose ever higher until it reached 168. Among the victims were nineteen children from a day-care center housed in the building.

After hearing about the children, Hartzler decided to get involved in the case. He immediately called a friend in the U.S. Justice Department and offered to help in any way he could. He wanted to bring the person or people responsible for the bombing to justice.

As an assistant U.S. attorney, Hartzler had considerable experience and great success prosecuting criminals. This experience could come in handy in what could well be the most publicized federal trial in decades. The Justice Department took Hartzler up on his offer. In May of 1995, Attorney General Janet Reno named Hartzler the lead prosecutor in the trial of suspected Oklahoma City bomber Timothy McVeigh.

The news media could not help but notice that the government's lead prosecutor in this blockbuster case used a motorized scooter to get around. Hartzler explained that this condition was a result of his MS.

Hartzler was born in 1950 in Columbus, Ohio, which belongs to that northern tier of states where MS is more common, and raised not far from there. His parents, who worked in the insurance business, provided him with a fairly typical middle-class upbringing. He led an active life and pursued his goals with tenacious energy. In 1972, Hartzler earned a degree from Amherst College in Massachusetts, and in 1978 he graduated first in his class in law school at American University in Washington, D.C.

For 10 years, Hartzler put his legal training to use as a federal prosecutor in Chicago. He gained widespread recognition for his sure handling of a case in which the government charged four Puerto Rican nationalists with conducting a terrorist bombing campaign. Hartzler obtained convictions against all four. Three were sent to prison and the fourth was given probation. Evenhanded in his pursuit of justice, Hartzler went after corrupt judges as well as society's misfits.

In the late 1980s, Hartzler began to experience a strange weakness in his legs. Doctors diagnosed the problem as MS in 1989. Hartzler was in his late thirties at the time— on the upper end of, but still within, the high-risk age range for MS. For a man who led a vigorous, active life, the news was a shock. Hartzler was the type of man who had once chased a purse snatcher through a crowded Chicago train station, tackled him, and held him in a headlock until the police arrived. Now he had to face some unpleasant realities. His symptoms were so severe that he quickly lost the ability to walk by himself. Hartzler, though, was determined to keep a positive focus. "I had to ask myself, 'What can I do?' Not focus on what I can't do," he said.[14]

One of the results of Hartzler's self-inventory was a decision to alter his lifestyle. This included cutting back on his relentless work schedule. Just before he began experiencing symptoms of MS, he had quit the U.S. Attorney's office to take a high-paying job with a prestigious law firm. As he reflected on how fleeting and precious life was, he decided that he did not want to spend so much of it driving to and from the office and working late into the evening. He missed spending time with his wife, Lisa, and resented being away from home so much while his three boys were growing up. After only 2 years at the firm, Hartzler startled colleagues by resigning and returning to work as an assistant U.S. attorney. This time he

Assistant U.S. Attorney Joseph Hartzler leaves the U.S. Federal Court House in Denver, Colorado, where Timothy McVeigh was put on trial.

joined the Springfield, Illinois, office rather than the Chicago office. He could reach his new office in 10 minutes.

When his sons joined a youth baseball league, Hartzler wanted to volunteer to help with the team. Before MS struck, he had thought about coaching the boys. Should he do it now even with his disabilities? Hartzler finally asked himself, "Would I do this if I didn't have MS?"[15] The answer was yes. Hartzler decided that MS itself posed enough limitations. He was not about to add to those restrictions by backing out of things he wanted to do and was capable of doing. So he signed on as coach.

He prowled around the baseball field on his motorized scooter, offering instructions and encouragement to his team. When the team was given black-and-white uniforms, Hartzler named them the "Mighty Skunks." It was Hartzler's private joke that the team's initials were the same as those of his disease.

Hartzler remained so active and enthusiastic during the 1990s that he was chosen as the Multiple Sclerosis Society's Father of the Year in 1995. He had little time to savor the award, however. At about the time it was presented to him, the U.S. Justice Department accepted his offer and named him lead prosecutor in the Oklahoma City bombing case. As with his decision to coach, Hartzler had to ponder the wisdom of taking on the assignment. It meant 2 years of intense work, emotional stress, and travel back and forth to Oklahoma City. In the end, he asked himself the same question as before, "Would I do this if I did not have MS?" Deciding that he would, Hartzler took on the challenge. "I thought I could make a difference," he said in describing his decision.[16]

In addition to doing his best to see that the bomber was brought to justice, one of Hartzler's main goals was to restore faith in and respect for the U.S. system of justice. Like millions of other observers, he had cringed at the undignified legal squabbling and prosecutorial mistakes that had marred the highly publicized O. J. Simpson murder trial. He wanted to show people that the American courts were not circus arenas and showplaces for celebrity-seeking lawyers, but halls of justice.

Upon the announcement of Hartzler as the lead prosecutor, the news media immediately focused on his disability. Some questioned whether he was up to the rigors of the job. Others speculated that the government had chosen a disabled man to appeal to the sympathy of the jury. Seasoned lawyers, however, knew that the government had simply chosen an outstanding prosecutor. Even defense attorneys who had opposed

Joseph Hartzler poses with his wife and three children outside their home in Springfield, Illinois. He was named Multiple Sclerosis Father of the Year in 1995.

him in court hailed the choice. "His integrity is beyond reproach," commented one. "He's a prosecutor I can turn my back on."[17]

Hartzler welcomed the media coverage as a chance to show the public that MS does not prevent a person from performing well in a demanding, high-profile job. He jokingly asked reporters if they were up to the physical demands of covering *him*. "You have to jog to keep up with me when I'm on the scooter," he said.[18]

One element of the press coverage bothered him, however. A caption under a photograph of him in a major news magazine said, "Hartzler suffers from multiple sclerosis." "I *have* MS," he explained. "I don't suffer from it."[19]

Hartzler prepared thoroughly for the prosecution of Timothy McVeigh. He spent 100 hours preparing one key witness for his testimony on the stand. Yet he took care to keep from overworking himself enough to provoke a flare-up.

At the trial, Hartzler avoided dramatic showmanship and blustering arguments. With his ability to make a complex case easily understandable, he constructed a solid wall of evidence against McVeigh. A soft-spoken man, Hartzler allowed others to share both the credit and the responsibilities. Closing arguments normally give center stage to the prosecutor, but Hartzler let one of his assistants handle that segment of the case.

One legal analyst summed up Hartzler's performance as "brilliant. I've never seen a prosecution put on as well as this one."[20] On June 2, 1997, the jury found McVeigh guilty of the bombing.

Hartzler took satisfaction in having done his best to serve his country and in demonstrating that people with MS can perform difficult tasks. "It could be a lot worse," Hartzler said when asked about his MS. "It's not fatal. It's not contagious." With his unsinkable sense of humor, he added, "I've learned that if you're going to be one of God's chosen, MS is not the worst."[21]

The Mysterious Ski-Slope Coincidence

Although raised in a different country, Jimmie Heuga has been friends with Egon Zimmerman and Josef Steigler for more than 30 years. It was a friendship forged in the fire of international competition. Skiing for the United States, Heuga won a bronze medal in the slalom event at the 1964 Winter Olympics in Innsbruck, Austria. Along with silver medalist William Kidd, the 20-year-old Heuga was the first American to win a medal in Olympic Alpine skiing.

At those Olympics, Heuga was chasing two heroes of the host country. Josef (Pepi) Steigler, a part-time photographer from Lienz, Austria, had been awarded a place on his country's ski team at the last minute. Steigler took advantage of his opportunity by capturing the gold medal in the slalom. Steigler's teammate, Egon Zimmerman, came from Lech, an Austrian mountain village that had been converted to a ski resort after World War I. Since his parents did not consider skiing a useful skill, he had learned a trade as a chef. But he, too, struck gold at Innsbruck. By winning the downhill competition, Zimmerman became the third person from his village of 200 people to win an Olympic gold medal.

The three men kept in touch with one other over the years. Incredibly, one-by-one, they all developed MS. Their stories demonstrate the mysterious, widely varying nature of the disease. Heuga experienced a bout of blurred vision at the age of 23—only 3 years after his Olympic success. Doctors were unable to determine the cause of the problem. A year later, he suddenly felt a strange numbness in his legs. This condition, too, went away after a brief time. But when his symptoms returned 2 years later in 1970, Heuga was diagnosed with MS.

Heuga's case was quite severe, and by 1975 he was having trouble coping with his illness. He gave up all activities and stayed at home, visiting no one. His attitude took its toll on his relationship with his wife, who divorced him.

One afternoon, Heuga finally took stock of himself. He realized that he could keep on feeling sorry for himself and

Josef Steigler, Jim Heuga, and Egon Zimmerman
became friends when they skied together in the 1964
Winter Olympics. Today, all three men have MS.

wasting his life in seclusion, or he could rejoin the living.
Heuga chose life. He worked himself back into shape through
swimming, biking, and other exercises, and eventually remar-
ried. Looking for ways to make himself useful, he lobbied for a
$10,000 grant to establish a fitness center in Avon, Colorado,
specifically to serve those with MS.

Heuga's disease grew progressively worse. By the mid-
1990s, he could move around only with the aid of a wheelchair and was not able to perform simple tasks, such as
getting himself a cup of coffee. But he remained upbeat.

"You can have a disease and still maintain the quality of your life," he says.[22]

Egon Zimmerman sympathized with his old friend for a long time. Then, some years after Heuga developed MS, Zimmerman began to experience mild problems with his coordination. He was diagnosed as having MS in 1987 at the age of 48. Unlike Heuga, Zimmerman has never had problems performing everyday activities. Except for a slightly stiff-legged walk, his MS is not even noticeable.

Still, Zimmerman remains self-conscious about his disease to the point where he has cut back his activity more than his physical disability demands. "I don't want to show that I'm not fit," he explained to a magazine reporter. "I have too much pride."[23]

Pepi Steigler thought it was a strange coincidence as he watched both of his former skiing competitors come down with the same disease. Steigler, who in 1965 had moved to the western United States to set up a ski school, was thankful that he remained healthy. Then in 1992, Steigler was out driving near his home in Wyoming when he experienced double vision. Although he was well beyond the age when MS usually strikes, Steigler, too, was diagnosed with the disease.

As with Zimmerman, Steigler's symptoms were not severe, and he, too, did his best to hide his lapses of coordination. But in March of 1994, his wife persuaded him to go public with his illness. Steigler found it liberating to openly acknowledge his situation. "I relate to people better now," he notes. "I've become more outgoing."[24]

The strange case of the three skiers only adds to the mystery over what causes MS. Statistically, there is nothing that links MS with skiing—skiers are no more likely than the average person to develop the disease—and science has established that the disease is not contagious. Other than bizarre coincidence, or the suggestion of an unknown environmental trigger, no one has been able to demonstrate why all three Olympic medalists would have developed a relatively rare disease.

Sweet Relief

Victoria Williams is not a music-world name that many people recognize. But her adoring fans include such high-powered entertainers as Neil Young and the members of Pearl Jam, making her one of the rare singers whose fans are more famous than she is.

Williams was born and raised in Louisiana, a relatively low-risk area for MS. Ever since starting piano lessons in third grade, she had been pointing herself toward a music career. Williams worked her way up slowly by singing in small clubs. In

Victoria Williams (left) on stage with Eddie Vedder (right) of Pearl Jam.

1987, the 27-year-old singer attracted enough notice to get her first album produced. Although her songs had limited play over the airwaves, she attracted a loyal following that included some of the biggest names in the industry.

In the spring of 1992, she traveled the country as a warm-up act for rock star Neil Young. When she took the stage at a concert in Detroit, she found herself strangely exhausted. She could not perform. As she described it, her fingers "were just flopping around and wouldn't do what my brain told them to do."[25] Frightened, the 32-year-old singer flew to her home in Los Angeles for tests. Doctors determined that she had MS.

In her first year of coping with the disease, Williams had such a severe flare-up that she lost the use of her legs. She was continually tired and could not get her fingers to play the piano up to her usual standards. Gradually, the worst symptoms faded away. Williams took to gardening to strengthen her fingers. She got used to dealing with her reduced energy level. But her MS had created a problem worse than the physical disabilities. As a self-employed singer, she had no medical insurance. The bills for the tests and treatments piled up until she was staring at a mountain of debt.

When her influential fans learned of her plight, though, they stepped in to help. In 1993, Pearl Jam and others recorded an album of Williams's songs in an effort to raise money for her. The album, called *Sweet Relief*, raised money as well as public awareness. Impressed by the songs on the album, producers offered Williams her own record contract. With her MS in remission, she completed a successful tour in 1995.

Reflecting on her roller coaster ride of emotions, Williams commented, "It just goes to show how something good can come out of something bad."[26]

The End of Life in the Fast Lane

Few people have bounced higher or crashed harder in their lives than comedian Richard Pryor. He struggled through a terrible childhood. Neglected by his parents, he grew up in

Comedian Richard Pryor performed in front of live audiences for many years.

Peoria, Illinois, in a house of prostitution run by his grandmother. His one saving gift was that he could make people laugh, a gift he first noticed when, as a child, he purposely fell off a porch railing to the delight of his audience.

Pryor used his sharp sense of humor to pull himself out of a world of poverty and crime. During the 1960s, he won acclaim as a sharper-edged alternative to another black comedian, Bill Cosby. By the 1970s, he reigned as one of the most popular entertainers in the United States. Pryor put out twenty comedy albums, appeared in forty films, and delivered his routine in hundreds of nightclubs.

In 1988, Richard Pryor (center) received the Mark Twain Prize. He is shown here on the way to the awards ceremony with his daughters Rain (left) and Elizabeth (right).

But he was unable to escape the wild, undisciplined habits he had formed in his youth. Pryor became addicted to drugs and achieved notoriety when he accidentally set himself on fire during one cocaine episode and nearly died from the burns.

Sobered by the experience and touched by the support of thousands of fans, Pryor settled down somewhat—although he was unable to completely escape the grip of substance abuse.

While continuing to perform as a comic in the 1980s, Pryor began to experience odd sensations in his muscles. As time went on, he began to tire easily, and he lost so much weight that some people suspected he had AIDS. Pryor simply pretended that the symptoms did not exist.

But one day in 1986 Pryor participated in a celebrity basketball game to raise money for charity. He was dribbling the ball when, without warning, he suddenly fell down. He had not slipped, nor had anyone bumped into him. It was just one of a series of events in which, as Pryor describes it, "My eyesight and balance came and went without informing me of [their] schedule."[27]

Bewildered and frightened by his inability to control his muscles, Pryor consulted doctors at the prestigious Mayo Clinic in Rochester, Minnesota. The diagnosis was MS.

Pryor flew back to his home in Los Angeles in shock. Neither he nor his wife mentioned the disease, and they made no plans for what to do next. Pryor mistakenly believed that the disease was the result of his unhealthy lifestyle. In some ways, he thought, he was getting what he deserved.

Over the course of the next several years, Pryor gradually learned to accept what had happened to him. He also realized that he would now, finally, have to start paying more attention to his health. The comedian slowed down his schedule and cut out the wild partying. He began exercising several times a week.

Speaking of his disease, Pryor acknowledged that he hated some of the limitations: for instance, his need, more and more, to use a wheelchair to get around. But he also found a positive side to his experience. "The heartbreak is out there, but it's not got me," he insisted.[28] Pryor has even toyed with the idea of incorporating MS into a stand-up comedy routine, although he has not yet figured out exactly how to do it.

Pryor admits that having MS has forced him to give up a dangerous lifestyle that he could not otherwise abandon. "It's a blessing, actually," he said of MS, "because if I didn't have this I'd be smoking it up."[29]

An Osmond Brother's Lonely Disease

Like Annette Funicello, Alan Osmond found entertainment stardom at an early age. At 11 years old, he was one of Utah's musical Osmond Brothers, who regularly performed on the Andy Williams television show in the 1960s. Later, he helped his even more talented younger siblings, Donny and Marie, launch their careers. Alan worked as a producer on their weekly television show and went on to direct a multimedia company.

Alan Osmond (second from left) and his brothers formed a popular musical group in the 1960s.

But over the years, he continued to perform off and on with his brothers, especially when the family opened up the Osmond Theater in Branson, Missouri.

In January 1987, Alan was playing the trumpet on stage when he found that his fingers could not press the valves on the instrument as fast as he wanted. At first, he was puzzled. Was he getting old? Was he just too tired to perform that night? Had he been slacking off on his practice so much that he could no longer meet the demands of his profession?

But as the problem persisted, Osmond began wondering if something more serious was happening. Had he suffered a stroke—a type of partial paralysis resulting from the brain being briefly deprived of oxygen? He decided to find out what was going on. The doctors ran him through a series of tests and finally diagnosed him with MS.

At the time, Osmond's only noticeable symptom was the weakness in his hand. But as the father of eight sons, he was forced to wonder how the disease might progress. How might it curtail his ability to parent? Osmond decided to face the issue head on, at least with his family. He told the boys, "I'm going to need your help, but I want you to be positive and make sure things don't change around here."[30]

Around most other people, however, Osmond did his best to keep the disease a secret. Like Annette Funicello, he was embarrassed by his lack of coordination and thought his fans would think less of him if they knew that he had MS. But over the years, his flare-ups produced additional symptoms that were increasingly difficult to disguise. He began to experience difficulty running and lifting his knees. Gradually, he developed a hitch in his walk.

In the fall of 1992, Osmond's arms and legs began to grow weaker. After stumbling several times, he got himself a foot brace for support. Next, he lost the ability to grip objects with his right hand. This made holding a pen impossible, so he learned to write with his left hand. His fingers grew so unresponsive that he could not even play chords on the piano. This last problem was especially discouraging. Alan used the piano to write songs for the Osmond Brothers.

Fortunately, he had a close-knit family to help out. He eventually learned to write songs with the aid of a son who played chords on a guitar as Alan called them out. His brothers, too, were happy to accommodate Alan's needs. Once at a show rehearsal, the brothers were practicing a song that demanded too much onstage movement for Alan to keep up with. Alan urged the brothers to go on without him. But instead, they simply changed the routine to something that Alan could handle. Episodes such as these have caused Alan to think of his MS as a partial blessing that has brought his family closer together.

In September 1994, after performing on a Jerry Lewis telethon to raise money for the fight against a disease called muscular dystrophy, Osmond was supposed to deliver a 30-second personal appeal for money. He had not planned to

Alan Osmond at home with his wife and children

reveal anything about his own illness, but as he thought about those who could be helped by medical research, he suddenly broke down. He knew what it was like to face a medical disability, he said, because he had multiple sclerosis. As soon as he got the words out, Osmond felt relief. Until that moment, he had never realized what a "lonely disease"[31] MS is when you are bearing the burden alone and keeping it a secret from others.

Like many other people with MS, Osmond has searched far and wide for a cure, or at least relief, from his symptoms. He has tried a number of experimental treatments as well as exercise programs in swimming pools and on trampolines. He regularly works with clay in an attempt to strengthen his fingers. He has, however, found no miracle cure. He continues to experience a decline in his body's efficiency. Holding a fork has become difficult, as has shaking hands. There is some paralysis on the right side of his body. Every so often, he longs for some of the physical activities he used to be able to do with ease, such as roughhousing with his kids.

So far, though, MS has not hindered his ability to get around. If it starts to, Osmond feels ready for that challenge. "If that day comes," he says, "I've got plenty of boys to lean on." Echoing Richard Pryor's determined attitude he says, "I have MS but MS, doesn't have me."[32]

Going the Distance

All her life, Moira Griffin had taken pride in being the most athletic girl she knew. So in 1983, when her legs started feeling shaky after a hard day of working in the horse stables, she refused to give them a rest. Instead, she mounted a horse and started off on a ride. A few minutes later, she began to lose her grip on the saddle as the horse cantered over a field. Griffin slid off and fell to the ground.

When a fellow rider asked what happened, Griffin had no answer. "I don't know," she said. "My legs are spaghetti."[33] Adding to her embarrassment was the fact that this was her third fall from a horse within just a few weeks. Finally convinced that she needed a break from her grueling physical labor, she quit her job as a stable groom and focused on becoming a freelance journalist.

But the thought that she could no longer handle rugged work nagged at her. Determined to redeem herself, she began training for a triathlon—a competition that combines long-distance running, biking, and swimming. To her puzzlement and despair, her running gait was awkward: she had trouble lifting her knees and her right foot struck the ground flat-footed. One day, she couldn't stop herself from running off a curb. When her legs suddenly buckled for no apparent reason, causing her to fall, Griffin knew she needed medical help.

After a CT scan revealed no brain tumor, further tests, including a spinal tap, placed the blame for her problems on MS. Griffin left the doctor's office in a state of shock. Like many people who suddenly find themselves diagnosed with a serious disease for which there is no known cause, she found herself full of anger. She blamed herself and her bad health habits. She blamed her breakup with a boyfriend. She blamed God. Thinking that her illness was a sign of a lack of willpower, she went on an exercise binge that only made her problems worse.

Griffin searched desperately for the miracle cure. She read everything she could get her hands on about MS cures, including material on acupuncture and special diets. After learning about the potential of a new substance called copolymer-1, she tried to enlist in tests of this new treatment. Unfortunately, she did not fit the requirements of the test group.

After fighting through depression, Griffin came to grips with the reality of MS. She decided to share the story of her struggles in an autobiographical book called *Going the Distance*. In it, she describes how she learned, with the support of family and friends, to regain control of her life, to live within her limits, and to feel compassion for others. "Griffin, it's not your fault that this has happened to you," she writes. "But you are responsible for the way you live with that disease."[34]

After being diagnosed with MS, Moira Griffin wrote a book called *Going the Distance.*

MS is a disease for which no cure has been found. It is unpredictable, ever changing, and in many ways, mysterious. It may get progressively worse over time, or it may not. MS most often affects young, healthy adults at their most productive time of life. As a result, the cost of dealing with the disease is enormous—in terms of work time and income lost as well as the physical and emotional burden it can place on people with the disease, their families, and their friends.

Medical researchers are just beginning to scratch the surface in their effort to understand what causes MS and their search for ways to treat and prevent the disease. The information they are uncovering provides hope that today's experiments will lead to effective treatments and prevention in the future.

In the meantime, the challenge for those living with MS is to deal with the disease in a positive manner. As Sarah Perry, a woman with MS, sums it up, "I learned that one never finishes adjusting to multiple sclerosis. I don't know why I thought one would. One does not, after all, finish adjusting to life, and MS is simply a fact of life."[35]

Glossary

allergy—an immune system overreaction against a harmless invading substance such as pollen or food

antibody—a protein produced by the body's immune system that attacks foreign bacteria, viruses, and toxins

antigen—the general name for any microorganism or toxin that invades the body

antigen-presenting cell (APC)—an immune system cell that travels through the body and identifies intruding antigens

autoimmune reaction—when the immune system mistakes body cells for antigens and attacks them

benign—a form of disease that produces no symptoms

computerized tomography (CT)—a test that compiles a series of X-ray photographs of the brain into a three-dimensional picture *corticosteroid*—one of a family of hormones that suppress the immune system's production of antibodies

electroencephalogram (EEG)—a test that measures electrical activity in the brain

flare-up—a period in which MS produces a flurry of symptoms

interferon—one of a family of proteins that is able to suppress certain autoimmune responses and is particularly effective in treating MS

magnetic resonance imaging (MRI)—a test that charts the variation in response to radio waves to give a clear picture of body tissues

major histocompatibility complex (MHC)—a group of genes that instruct cells to manufacture proteins that help T-cells distinguish between body cells and antigens

myelin—a material made of fat and protein that serves as insulation around nerve fibers

nerve fiber—stringy material that connects muscles and sensory organs to the brain and spinal cord

neurologist—a physician who specializes in the treatment of the nervous system

oral tolerization—a technique of ingesting antigens to build up the body's tolerance to a substance. In MS, the technique is viewed as a possible way to get the immune system to stop attacking myelin.

plaque—a damaged piece of myelin that forms a hardened patch around a nerve fiber *primary progressive multiple sclerosis*—a form of MS in which the symptoms become steadily more severe over time

relapsing-progressive multiple sclerosis—a form of MS in which the unpredictable attacks gradually produce more severe symptoms

relapsing-remitting multiple sclerosis—a form of MS in which the symptoms go through a cycle of appearing, subsiding, reappearing, subsiding, and so on

renegade T-cell—a faulty immune system cell that cannot distinguish body cells from antigens

surface marker—a molecule on the surface of an invading agent that identifies a microorganism or toxin to antibodies

T-cell—a white blood cell that attacks or aids the immune system's attack against antigens

Bibliography

Aaseng, Nathan. *Autoimmune Diseases*. New York: Franklin Watts, 1995.

Anderson, Peter-Brian, et al. "How Shall We Proceed with Disease-Modification Treatments for MS?" *Lancet*, 1 March 1997.

"Annette's Dream . . . Raising Public Awareness about MS." *Inside MS*, Summer 1994.

Black, Pamela. "Turning Off Renegade T-Cells." *Business Week*, 15 November 1991.

Bylinsky, Gene. "The New Attack on Killer Diseases." *Fortune*, 22 April 1991.

Carrol, David L., and Jon Dudley Dorman. *Living Well with Multiple Sclerosis*. New York: Harper, 1993.

"The Challenge of His Life." *People Weekly*, 16 October 1995.

Cohen, Jon. "Mounting a Targeted Strike on Unwanted Immune Response." *Science,* 7 August 1992.

Collins, James. "The Burden of Proof." *Time,* 26 May 1997.

George-Warren, Holly. "Forever Mickey's Girl." *New York Times,* 21 November 1993.

Grady, Denise. "Experts Ask Why So Few Take Drugs for M.S." *New York Times,* 8 June 1999.

"Hope for M.S.—If Cell Grafts Stick." *Business Week,* 20 January 1997.

"In Case You Hadn't Heard." *Alcoholism & Drug Abuse Weekly,* 10 July 1995.

Kastilahn, Kathleen. "Good Job, Joe." *Lutheran,* August 1997.

Kent, Debra. "Hoping for a Miracle." *McCalls,* June 1994.

MacFarlane, Ellen Burstein. "My Doctor Duped Me." *Ladies Home Journal,* January 1996.

Marx, Jean. "Testing of Autoimmune Therapy Begins." *Science,* 5 April 1991.

"The Music of Hope." *People Weekly,* 1 May 1995.

"Nowhere to Hide." *People Weekly,* 29 May 1995.

Perry, Sarah. *Living with Multiple Sclerosis: A Personal Account of Coping and Adapting.* Hants, England: Aldershot, 1994.

Plummer, William, et al. "The Enemy Within." *People Weekly,* 13 November 1995.

Prater, Merle P., and Walter B. Eidbo. "Ionizing Radiation: The Long Sought Environmental Trigger for Multiple Sclerosis?" Self-published, 1994.

Pryor, Richard with Todd Gold. "Pryor Convictions." *Ebony*, September 1995.

Sibley, William. *Therapeutic Claims in Multiple Sclerosis.* New York: Demos, 1992.

Sternberg, S. "New Multiple Sclerosis Drug Clears Hurdle." *Science News*, 28 September 1996.

"A Sweetheart in Autumn." *People Weekly*, 23 October 1995.

Terry, Don. "Steel With Soft Surface." *New York Times*, 3 July, 1997.

Travis, J. "It's Genes, Not a Virus." *Science News*, 16 September 1995.

"With Faith to Carry On." *People Weekly*, 19 June 1995.

Wolfe, Yun Lee. "Rx for MS." *Prevention*, June 1997.

End Notes

Chapter 1
1. Holly George-Warren, "Forever Mickey's Girl," *New York Times,* 21 November 1993, p. 9.
2. "A Sweetheart in Autumn," *People Weekly,* 23 October 1995, p. 111.
3. Annette Funicello with Patricia Romanowski, *A Dream Is a Wish Your Heart Makes* (New York: Hyperion, 1994), p. 170.
4. George-Warren, "Forever Mickey's Girl," p. 1.
5. "Annette's Dream . . . Raising Public Awareness about MS," *Inside MS,* Summer 1994, p. 9.

Chapter 3
6. Debra Kent. "Hoping for a Miracle," *McCalls,* June 1994, p. 116.

Chapter 4
7. J. Travis. "It's Genes, Not a Virus," *Science News,* 16 September 1995, p. 180.

Chapter 6

8. Funicello, *Dream*, p.187.
9. S. Sternberg, "New Multiple Sclerosis Drug Clears Hurdle," *Science News*, 28 September 1996, p. 199.
10. Denise Grady, "Experts Ask Why So Few Take Drugs for M.S.," *New York Times*, 8 June 1999, p. F7.
11. Gene Bylinsky, "The New Attack on Killer Diseases," *Fortune*, 22 April 1991, p. 181.
12. Richard Lechtenberg, *The Multiple Sclerosis Fact Book* (Philadelphia: F. A. Davis, 1995), p. 9.

Chapter 7

13. Ellen Burstein MacFarlane, "My Doctor Duped Me," *Ladies Home Journal*, January 1996, p. 40.
14. Kathleen Kastilahn, "Good Job, Joe," *Lutheran*, August 1997, p. 24.
15. Kastilahn, "Good Job, Joe," p. 24.
16. Don Terry, "Steel With Soft Surface," *New York Times*, 3 July 1997, p. A19.
17. Terry, "Steel," p. A19.
18. Kastilahn, "Good Job, Joe," p. 24.
19. Kastilahn, "Good Job, Joe," p. 24.
20. James Collins, "The Burden of Proof," *Time*, 26 May 1997, p. 32.
21. "The Challenge of His Life," *People Weekly*, 16 October 1995, p. 170.
22. William Plummer, et al. "The Enemy Within," *People Weekly*, 13 November 1995, p. 156.
23. Plummer, "Enemy," p. 156.
24. Plummer, "Enemy," p. 156.
25. "The Music of Hope," *People Weekly*, 1 May 1995, p. 79.
26. "The Music of Hope," p. 79.
27. Richard Pryor with Todd Gold, "Pryor Convictions," *Ebony*, September 1995, p. 92.
28. "Nowhere to Hide," *People Weekly*, 29 May 1995, p. 77.

29. "In Case You Hadn't Heard," *Alcoholism & Drug Abuse Weekly*, 10 July 1995, p. 6.
30. "With Faith to Carry On," *People Weekly*, June 19, 1995, p. 74
31. "With Faith to Carry On," p. 74.
32. "With Faith to Carry On," p. 73.
33. Moira Griffin, *Going the Distance: Living a Full Life with Multiple Sclerosis and Other Debilitating Diseases* (New York: Dutton, 1989), p. 10.
34. Griffin, *Going the Distance*, p. 75.
35. Sarah Perry, *Living With Multiple Sclerosis: A Personal Account of Coping and Adapting* (Hants, England: Aldershot, 1994), p. 59.

For More Information

Books

Aaseng, Nathan. *Autoimmune Diseases.* Danbury, CT: Franklin Watts, 1995.

Cristall, Barbara. *Coping When a Parent Has MS.* New York: Rosen, 1992.

Funicello, Annette, with Patricia Romanowski. *A Dream Is a Wish Your Heart Makes.* New York: Hyperion, 1994.

Griffin, Moira. *Going the Distance: Living a Full Life with Multiple Sclerosis and Other Debilitating Diseases.* New York: Dutton, 1989.

Hyde, Margaret O., and Elizabeth Forsyth. *The Disease Book: A Kid's Guide.* New York: Walker, 1997.

Isler, Charlotte, and Alywyn T. Cohall, M.D. *The Watts Teen Health Dictionary.* Danbury, CT: 1996.

Lechtenberg, Richard. *The Multiple Sclerosis Fact Book.* Philadelphia: F. A. Davis, 1995.

Parker, Steve. *The Brain and Nervous System.* Danbury, CT: Franklin Watts, 1990.

Rosner, Louis, and Shelly Ross. *Multiple Sclerosis: New Hope and Practical Advice for People with MS and Their Families.* New York: Simon & Schuster, 1992.

Organizations and Online Sites

The Multiple Sclerosis Foundation
6350 N. Andrews Avenue
Fort Lauderdale, FL 33309
http//www.msfacts.org
This site features toll-free phone numbers for support lines, an MS library, MS updates, and other material.

The National Multiple Sclerosis Society
73 Third Avenue
New York, NY 10017
http://www.nmss.org
This site offers information, updates on current research, and other resources.

The National Institute of Neurological Disorders and Stroke
P.O. Box 5801
Bethesda, MD 20824
http://www.ninds.nih.gov
The institute has a free 20-page guide to MS. Its Web site offers additional material on MS.

Index

About the Author

NATHAN AASENG is the author of more than 140 books for young readers. As former research microbiologist, he is uniquely qualified to write books on a variety of health topics. Some of his most recent titles include *Cerebral Palsy, Autoimmune Diseases, Colds and Flu,* and *Head Injuries.* He lives in Eau Claire, Wisconsin, with his wife and four children.